The Constitution

by David Niecikowski

Illustrated by Kathryn Marlin

Cover by Jeff Van Kanegan

Publisher
Instructional Fair • TS Denison
Grand Rapids, MI 49455

About the Author

David Niecikowski has taught elementary, middle, and high school. He holds dual certification in Elementary and Secondary Social Studies and is currently acquiring a Master's degree in instructional technology. In addition to his current job as a ninth grade world history/geography teacher, David tutors, writes, programs, and plays music. David also enjoys spending time with his wife, Julie, and son, Edward, in their Tucson home.

Instructional Fair • TS Denison grants the individual purchaser permission to reproduce the student activity materials in this book for noncommercial individual or classroom use only. Reproduction for an entire school or school system is strictly prohibited. No part of this publication may be reproduced for storage in a retrieval system, or transmitted in any form or by any means, electronic, mechanical, recording, or otherwise, without the prior written permission of the publisher. For information regarding permission, write to Instructional Fair • TS Denison, P.O. Box 1650, Grand Rapids, MI 49501.

ISBN: 1-56822-634-9
The Constitution
Copyright © 1998 by Instructional Fair • TS Denison
2400 Turner Avenue NW
Grand Rapids, Michigan 49544

All Rights Reserved • Printed in the USA

TABLE OF CONTENTS

Constitutional History
Why Study the United States Constitution? 1
Pre-Colonial Background 2
Pre-Revolution Background 3
Revolution, Independence, and First Government 4
Steps to a New Government 5
Approving the New Government 6

The United States Constitution
How the Constitution Is Organized 7
Preamble 7
Article I 8
How a Bill Becomes Law 16
The Powers of Congress 17
Article II 23
Article III 26
The United States System of Government 28
Article IV 30
Articles V and VI 32
Article VII 33

Amendments to the Constitution
Amendments 1-4 34
Amendments 5-10 36
Amendments 11-13 38
Amendment 14 40
Amendments 15-18 42
Amendments 19-20 44
Amendments 21-23 46
Amendments 24-25 48
Amendments 26-27 50
Practice Tests 51
Answer Key 58

ABOUT THIS BOOK

Through easy-to-read activities and explanations, this book will assist students in understanding the most important details and concepts of the U.S. Constitution and the government it created. Whether learning about the Constitution for the first time or looking for an effective and complete resource to shed some light on unanswered questions, several features are included that can help make comprehending the Constitution a successful and pleasant experience:

- A handy Table of Contents section allows students to skip to sections for quick review.

- Over 200 vocabulary words are defined to help students overcome the Constitution's intimidating vocabulary and complex sentence structure.

- Historical Background sections illuminate students' questions as to why and how the nation's highest laws were drafted.

- Combined with the included original text of the Constitution, Know the Facts sections emphasize and teach the Constitution's critical concepts and improve technical reading and thinking skills.

- Challenging Practice Tests at the end of the book are provided to test and reinforce students' comprehension and attainment of the facts.

- An answer key is included to provide immediate feedback on all questions students are asked to answer.

Why Study the United States Constitution?

"Because I have to," is a reason, but one of the best reasons comes from Thomas Jefferson who once said that a nation cannot be both ignorant and free. In other words, if you do not know what freedoms you have and why you have them, then you are helpless in preventing your freedoms from being taken away. The Constitution defines and protects our freedoms and how our government operates on these freedoms. To know our government is to understand how your life is affected by it, and with this knowledge you have what it takes to make informed decisions in our democracy.

WHAT IS A DEMOCRACY?
The word *democracy* comes from the Greek words *demos* and *kratos*. *Demos* means "people" and *kratos* means "power," "authority," or "rule." Thus, a democracy is a type of government in which the people have the power to make the rules/laws directly or elect representatives to make laws for them. The U.S. Constitution guarantees a representative or indirect national democracy because we elect representatives, senators, and through electors, the president, to make national decisions and laws for us. However, as in the old Greek city states, some U.S. states and cities allow the people to directly create and vote on their own local laws.

WHAT IS A CONSTITUTION?
A written constitution is a set of rules that describe a government's purpose, principles, powers, limits, organization, and relationship between the government and the people governed. Like rules to a board or card game, a constitutional form of government has its most important rules listed in its constitution (the rule book) that limit what the government (controlled by people who play and run the game) can and cannot do. The U.S. government must obey the rules of the Constitution, which can only be changed through representatives chosen and thus, indirectly approved, by people who can vote in the United States.

WHO MADE THE CONSTITUTION AND WHY?
The framers (George Washington, Benjamin Franklin, James Madison, William Paterson, Edmund Randolph, and Roger Sherman, to name a few) made history when they drafted the oldest constitution written for a national government still active today. They based many of the Constitution's ideas upon historical observations, events, and experiences. Events on the next four pages are organized under four historical categories. The events are in order but the descriptions of the events are not. See if you can match each description to its correct event. Read carefully for ordering clues by paying attention to dates and subject references.

PRE-COLONIAL BACKGROUND

Place the letter of the correct description in the blank beside the answer. The first one has been completed.

1. __E__ Greek City States
2. _____ Roman Empire
3. _____ Magna Carta
4. _____ Petition of Right
5. _____ English Bill of Rights
6. _____ Natural Law

A. About 2,000 years ago this culture, borrowing ideas from the Greeks, elected people to pass laws and run the government for them. It had a republican form of government which existed to help everyone and not just one person, such as a king.

B. The English once again had to make their king sign this document, guaranteeing that taxes could only be collected if Parliament (made up of nobles and land owners who advised the king) agreed that there would be no forced housing of troops in people's homes and that no one could be imprisoned without a trial. This occurred 413 years after the Magna Carta. The document also said that even a king must obey the laws.

C. Witnessing and reflecting on historical abuses of power by monarchs (kings and queens) during the seventeenth and eighteenth centuries, European philosophers, particularly John Locke, promoted the idea, that the people have the right to control their own government and that only the people (not a king) can give and take away power from the government. Since government exists to protect life, freedom, and property, the people have the right to make a new government when the old government fails in its duty to protect the people.

D. In 1689 Parliament took more power away from monarchs by guaranteeing the following rights in this document: right of free elections, petitioning the king, speedy trials, no unfair bail (payment by the accused to be released from prison until the date of the trial), no unusual or cruel punishment, keeping an army in times of peace, and keeping and carrying weapons.

E. About 2,500 years ago free males from the city of Athens met to discuss and pass laws. Like many democracies that would follow, about half of this culture's population (women and slaves) could not participate in this culture's government.

F. After the fall of the Roman Empire, individuals rose to power as kings and queens (monarchs) to protect their people from barbarian tribes. In return for this protection, most of the people had to give up many of their rights, such as a voice in what laws could be passed. After 700 years of government by all-powerful monarchs, English noblemen limited the power of their king by making him sign this document in 1215, which guaranteed independent courts, trial by jury, and protection from unnecessary searches, loss of life, and loss of property.

Pre-Revolution Background

Place the letter of the correct description in the blank beside the answer.

1. _____ The Great Peace
2. _____ House of Burgesses
3. _____ Mayflower Compact
4. _____ The Albany Plan of Union
5. _____ Stamp Act Congress

A. On November 11, 1620, before setting foot on land with no government to guarantee fairness and individual rights, 41 Pilgrim males signed this agreement promising to make and obey all needed laws for their colony. This was the first written constitution in North America and another important step toward establishing self-government in the English colonies.

B. Before Europeans settled North America, five Native-American tribes, located in what would be today's northeastern part of the United States, joined together in an event to end conflict among themselves and to protect one another from common enemies. This confederation of tribes, called the Iroquois League, had a democratic government based on an oral constitution that outlined procedures for a representative council to make decisions for the entire league. Evidence suggests that the league's ideas of governing influenced the shaping of the Articles of Confederation and the U.S. Constitution.

C. Fighting a war with the French and their Indian allies in 1754, Benjamin Franklin proposed the idea that each of the 13 colonies send delegates (representatives) to an annual congress to raise money and pay for an army to defend the colonies. The congress would also have the power to settle border disputes, make treaties, and set up rules for trade with Indians. However, not wanting to give up any of their power, the British government and the colonial legislatures turned down the idea.

D. In an effort to improve profits in England's first permanent colony, the Virginia Company allowed Jamestown's males to own land and to vote for representatives in what would become Europe's first representative law-making body in the New World. Most importantly, this representative assembly, founded in 1619, helped establish the idea of self-government (that people have the right to rule themselves) in the other 12 English colonies that would follow.

E. Defeating the French cost England a great deal of money. To earn back their money, Parliament passed a law in 1765 requiring colonists to buy stamps on all legal documents. Because the colonies were not allowed to have representatives in Parliament, they cried "taxation without representation!" Delegates from nine colonies met in New York and formed this assembly and sent the king a petition telling him the tax was unfair. This was the first time that a large number of colonies united to protest actions by England's government.

Revolution, Independence, and First Government

Place the letter of the correct description in the blank beside the answer.

1. _____ Continental Association
2. _____ Common Sense
3. _____ Declaration of Independence
4. _____ Articles of Confederation

A. As in the past, the English government ignored the colonies' requests stated in the Declaration of Rights and reacted harshly by making stricter laws. In 1775 colonial militias and the British armies clashed at Concord, Lexington, and Bunker Hill. Tired of English abuses and with the recent battles showing that the colonial militias could hold their own against the British army, Thomas Paine wrote this pamphlet persuasively calling for the colonies to separate from England and replace rule by monarchs with a democratic rule by the people.

B. After declaring independence, the Second Continental Congress drafted this constitution in 1777 to unite the states under one government. It was not until the American Revolution was almost over that the last of the 13 states agreed to the new government in 1781. Not wanting to be told what to do by monarchs or have an excessively strong central government like Parliament, the document allowed each of the 13 states to maintain its independence as if each were a separate country. There was a national Congress, but some of its only powers included making war and peace, borrowing money, raising a national army and navy, making treaties with foreign governments, and settling disputes between the states who were only united by "a firm league of friendship." Since Congress had no power to tax and could only borrow money, it was weak in power, especially when the states refused to fund and obey the laws passed by Congress. States violated the Constitution's laws and made treaties with foreign governments. They raised armies, made their own money with little backing, and made it hard to trade with one another since Congress had no power to make rules guaranteeing fair trade.

C. When Parliament continued to tax the colonies and pass hated laws, and after such events as the Boston Massacre and the Boston Tea Party, delegates from the colonies met as the First Continental Congress in 1774. They adopted this document which, for the first time, united the colonies to act against England. They drafted another document, the Declaration of Rights, and sent it to King George III to inform him that the colonies would refuse to buy British goods until Parliament changed its laws. Unlike the Albany Plan, every colonial legislature approved the Continental Congress' actions.

D. The Second Continental Congress asked Thomas Jefferson to draft this document informing King George III that the United States of America (the former 13 colonies) was free and independent from England on July 4, 1776. The reason, Jefferson writes, is that King George III has been a cruel and unjust king who has ignored "natural law." Still believing that the colonies' only purpose was to serve England, the king would not let the colonies go free without a fight. This fight became known as the American Revolution.

STEPS TO A NEW GOVERNMENT

Place the letter of the correct description in the blank beside the answer.

1. ____ Constitutional Convention
2. ____ Virginia and New Jersey Plans
3. ____ The Connecticut or Great Compromise
4. ____ Slave Compromises

A. Another argument emerged to threaten the success of the convention. The Northern states wanted to outlaw slavery, but the Southern states successively argued that they needed slaves to make a living. A series of deals were made to prevent Southern states from leaving the convention and the Union. Because the Southern states had fewer free people than the Northern states, every five slaves would count as three people when counting population towards the number of representatives in the House. Despite this formula, the anti-slave North could still outvote the South in Congress, so it was written into the Constitution that the new Congress could not outlaw the shipping of slaves into the United States before 1808. Finally, Southern states had it written into the Constitution that fugitive, escaped slaves must be returned to their owners.

B. Arguments over representation in Congress almost brought the convention to an end. There was even talk of creating two separate countries. But the delegates from this small state held the convention together when they proposed an idea that both sides accepted. Borrowing from the Virginia Plan, the lower house of Congress, the House of Representatives, would have representation based on state population. Borrowing from the New Jersey Plan, the upper house of Congress, the Senate, would have equal representation, giving each state two senators.

C. Early in the convention, delegates from this large state introduced a proposal that helped convince the delegates to give up on the Articles of Confederation for a new federal/national government that would have the power to make the states obey its laws. The legislative department/Congress would make all national laws as the first branch of the federal government, and the judiciary department would settle arguments over national laws and hear appeals from state courts as the third branch. A new position of president would be created to execute/enforce national laws as the second branch. Delegates from this smaller state called for similar ideas in their proposal but greatly disagreed with the larger state's proposal that representation in Congress be based on population rather than representation equally divided among the states. Representation by population would have allowed the more populous, larger states to control Congress.

D. Under the Articles of Confederation the states had too much power, and the weak central government (Congress) was helpless in checking this power. In 1787 all states but one sent delegates to this event in Philadelphia to fix the articles' problems. Their representatives would quickly agree that the articles were too flawed to fix and that a new government, a much stronger central government, was needed to use its increased powers to truly unite the 13 states as one nation by passing and enforcing laws that would equally protect all its states and citizens.

APPROVING THE NEW GOVERNMENT

After 39 delegates from 12 states signed the document outlining a federal system of government, copies of the United States Constitution were sent to the 13 states on September 28, 1787, for approval. Any proposed changes to the current government under the Articles of Confederation required all 13 states to agree. But this was one of the weaknesses of the articles because it made it too difficult to get anything done. Therefore, the framers wrote into the Constitution that only 9 out of 13 states needed to approve the Constitution, allowing the new federal government to begin, ending government under the Articles of Confederation.

Even though 11 states approved the Constitution by 1789, it was not until May 29, 1790, when the last state ratified the Constitution, almost a year after the new government had begun on March 4, 1789. The fight for ratification was not easy. The Anti-Federalists, those opposed to the proposed government, thought that life under the federal government would result in oppression by the rich, that it took too much power and rights away from the states, and that it failed to guarantee individual rights. The Federalists, (those in favor of ratification), won over enough voters with a series of newspaper articles called *The Federalist* papers. They argued that the Articles of Confederation were weak and that a federal system of government, which divided power between the central government and the states under a constitution, was the best way to govern. They also promised that the first job of the new Congress would be to propose amendments to the Constitution guaranteeing individual rights. They kept their promise by proposing the Bill of Rights.

THE CONSTITUTION IS A LIVING DOCUMENT

In about 7,000 words, the U.S. Constitution outlines a constitutional-federal plan for government that has been flexible enough for over 200 years to allow our nation to survive these many turning points: a farming-based to factory-based economy, from horses to trains and cars, the Civil War, two World Wars, the advent of nuclear and computer technology, and the civil rights movement. As you read about the Constitution, you will develop an understanding of why the Constitution is a living document today. The framers knew it was not perfect and, consequently, designed it to meet the needs of future generations through change (amendments). Each amendment has a history behind why it was needed, often to guarantee people's individual rights or protection from abuses of power. The original language of the Constitution was drafted with this in mind. Having just fought a cruel, abusive, and oppressive king, the framers were fearful of creating a national government with too much power and knew that our nation could only survive future abuses of power with a system of checks and balances and separation of powers. Despite its current and historical flaws, you will further develop the sense of why many believe the U.S. Constitution is one of the greatest documents of all time and that through this document, the United States has risen to become one of the greatest nations in human history.

How the Constitution Is Organized

The Constitution has seven articles and 27 amendments. Articles separate major topics, and amendments add or change the original Constitution's intent. Articles are further divided into sections, which list separate ideas within an article's topic. Numbers attached to paragraphs of a section are called clauses and are not part of the original Constitution but have been added for reference purposes. Words that have been crossed out represent language that no longer applies due to an amendment. Italicized words represent words that have no importance today. And words in bold represent difficult terms defined by this study guide.

PREAMBLE

We the people of the United States, in order to form a more perfect **union**[1], **establish justice**[2], insure domestic **tranquility**[3], provide for the common **defense**[4], promote the general **welfare**[5], and secure the blessings of liberty to ourselves and our **posterity**[6], do ordain and establish this Constitution for the United States of America.

The introduction to the Constitution tells two important things:
1. The Constitution was created by "We the people" and, therefore, serves the people;
2. It lists six reasons or purposes for the existence of the Constitution.

Match each reason, superscripted with a number above, with its correct explanation as shown in the first example:

__3__ A. To make a peaceful community

_____ B. To serve the people's needs

_____ C. To have more cooperation between the states (Remember the failures under the Articles of Confederation.)

_____ D. To defend the nation

_____ E. To make certain all future Americans are free to choose

_____ F. To have justice

Article I

Section 1

All **legislative**[1] powers herein granted shall be **vested**[2] in a **Congress**[3] of the United States, which shall consist of a Senate and House of Representatives.

Section 2

(1.) The House of Representatives shall be **composed**[4] of members chosen every second year by the people of the several states, and the **electors**[5] in each state shall have the **qualifications**[6] **requisite**[7] for electors of the most numerous **branch**[8] of the state legislature.

(2.) No person shall be a **representative**[9] who shall not have **attained**[10] to the age of twenty-five years, and been seven years a citizen of the United States, and who shall not, when elected, be an **inhabitant**[11] of that state in which he shall be chosen.

(3.) Representatives and direct taxes shall be apportioned among the several states which may be included within this Union, according to their respective numbers, ~~which shall be determined by adding to the whole number of free persons, including those bound to service for a term of years, and excluding Indians not taxed, three-fifths of all other persons~~. The actual **enumeration**[12] shall be made within three years after the first meeting of the Congress of the United States, and within every subsequent term of ten years, in such manner as they shall by law direct. The number of representatives shall not exceed one for every thirty thousand, but each state shall have at least one representative; *and until such enumeration shall be made, the state of New Hampshire shall be entitled to choose 3, Massachusetts 8, Rhode Island and Providence Plantations 1, Connecticut 5, New York 6, New Jersey 4, Pennsylvania 8, Delaware 1, Maryland 6, Virginia 10, North Carolina 5, South Carolina 5, and Georgia 3.*

(4.) When **vacancies**[13] happen in the representation from any state, the executive authority **thereof**[14] shall issue **writs**[15] of election to fill such vacancies.

(5.) The House of Representatives shall choose their **speaker**[16] and other officers; and shall have the **sole**[17] power of **impeachment**[18].

Historical Background

The Greeks practiced a form of impeachment called eisangelia, and the English helped spread the practice around the world. To date, the House of Representatives has used its impeachment power 16 times, but the Senate has only convicted 7 of those charges, all of which were federal judges. Of the last two removed in 1989, one was found guilty of accepting a bribe, and the other inappropriately helped a friend's son who was involved in a drug case. In 1805 Supreme Court Justice Samuel Chase was charged, but not convicted, and President Andrew Johnson came within one Senate vote of being removed from office in 1868. President Richard Nixon resigned (left office) in 1974 before the House took a vote to decide whether to impeach him.

VOCABULARY MATCHING

Look at Article I, Sections 1 and 2 for the words in bold with numbers next to them. Match each word in bold to its definition below by placing the word's number in the correct space as shown in the first example.

A. __10__ reached

B. _____ made up of

C. _____ house

D. _____ openings

E. _____ only, exclusive

F. _____ law-making

G. _____ resident (where live)

H. _____ given

I. _____ required

J. _____ legislating body

K. _____ court order

L. _____ voters

M. _____ to accuse a federal official of a crime or wrongdoing

N. _____ person who leads and keeps order in the House of Representatives

O. _____ count

P. _____ eligibility

Q. _____ law maker elected to the U.S. House of Representatives

R. _____ of that

Know the Facts

Read the text from the Constitution in Article I, Sections 1 and 2 and answer the following fill-in-the-blank questions using the list of answers. The questions follow the text in order. As an example, the first one has been completed.

A. two years
B. 25 years
C. make laws
D. seven years
E. Senate
F. House of Representatives
G. one representative
H. ten years
I. impeachment
J. representatives
K. resident

1. The power or job of Congress is to __C__.

2. The two houses of the bicameral legislature are the _____ and the _____.

3. Members of the House of Representatives are elected every _____.

4. A representative must be at least _____ old.

5. A representative must be a citizen of the United States for at least _____ and a _____ of the state from which he or she was elected to represent.

6. Population is counted every _____ to calculate the number of _____ each state gets in the House.

7. Each state is guaranteed at least _____.

8. The House of Representatives has the power to charge public officials of wrongdoing, which is otherwise known as the power of _____.

NOTES:
The first part of the crossed out language in clause 3 was made invalid by Amendment 16 allowing for a national income tax. With Amendments 13 and 14 outlawing slavery and giving African Americans equal protection of the laws, the 3/5 compromise was made obsolete. The reference to "Indians taxed" is also invalid because all Native Americans pay taxes in some way and all native-born are U.S. citizens as of 1924.

In 1929, Congress set the maximum number of representatives at 435. This means the average representative represents over 500,000 people from his or her state district. With increased population, the language (in italics) became outdated.

Vocabulary Matching

Match the words in bold on this page to their definitions below by placing the word's number in the correct space as shown in the first example.

A. __2__ result, effect
B. _____ for the time being
C. _____ promise to tell truth before God
D. _____ law maker elected to the U.S. Senate
E. _____ agreement
F. _____ left, forfeited
G. _____ criminal charges
H. _____ legally responsible
I. _____ examine by trial
J. _____ pledge to seriously state the truth
K. _____ found guilty
L. _____ positions held
M. _____ control (the trial)
N. _____ distinction (usually an unpaid job)
O. _____ end

Section 3

(1.) The Senate of the United States shall be composed of two **senators**[1] from each state, ~~chosen by the legislature thereof~~, for six years; and each senator shall have one vote.

(2.) Immediately after they shall be assembled in **consequence**[2] of the first election, they shall be divided as equally as may be into three classes. The **seats**[3] of the senators of the first class shall be **vacated**[4] at the **expiration**[5] of the second year, of the second class at the expiration of the fourth year, and of the third class at the expiration of the sixth year, so that one-third may be chosen every second year; ~~and if vacancies happen by resignation, or otherwise, during the recess of the legislature of any state, the executive thereof may make temporary appointments until the next meeting of the legislature, which shall then fill such vacancies~~.

(3.) No person shall be a senator who shall not have attained to the age of thirty years, and been nine years a citizen of the United States, and who shall not, when elected, be an inhabitant of that state for which he shall be chosen.

(4.) The Vice-President of the United States shall be president of the Senate, but shall have no vote, unless they be equally divided.

(5.) The Senate shall choose their other officers, and also a president *pro tempore*[6], in the absence of the Vice-President, or when he shall exercise the office of President of the United States.

(6.) The Senate shall have the sole power to **try**[7] all impeachments. When sitting for that purpose, they shall be on **oath**[8] or **affirmation**[9]. When the President of the United States is tried, the Chief Justice shall **preside**[10]: and no person shall be **convicted**[11] without the **concurrence**[12] of two-thirds of the members present.

(7.) Judgment in cases of impeachment shall not extend further than to removal from office, and disqualification to hold and enjoy any office of **honor**[13], trust or profit under the United States: but the party convicted shall nevertheless be **liable**[14] and subject to **indictment**[15], trial, judgment and punishment, according to law.

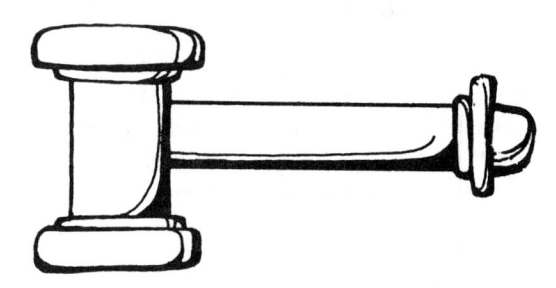

Know the Facts

Read the text from the Constitution in Article I, Sections 3 and answer the following fill-in-the-blank questions using the list of answers. One answer will be used more than once. The questions follow the text in order. As an example, the first one has been completed.

- A. 30
- B. One third
- C. resident
- D. two-thirds
- E. 6
- F. 9
- G. president pro tempore
- H. 2
- I. vice president
- J. second
- K. break ties
- L. impeachments

Historical Background

Impeachment Explained

Congress has the power to remove federal officials from office. The House of Representatives starts the two-step process by deciding whether to impeach/accuse the official of treason, bribery, or other crime. A majority vote is all that is needed to start the second step (Section 2, clause 5).

Once impeached, the Senate acts like a court and judges the official. The chief justice of the Supreme Court will judge a president brought to trial. A two-thirds Senate vote to convict is needed to remove any official from office (Section 3, clause 6).

Since a vote of guilty results only in a removal from office, a separate trial by a court of law would have to take place to determine any criminal punishment. In other words, Congress could remove a person from office on the grounds of misconduct, but a court of law could later find that same person innocent of criminal wrongdoing (Section 3, clause 7).

Unlike representatives who cast votes for the state districts which elected them, each of the (1) __H__ senators from a state represents ALL the people in that state for a term of (2)_____ years. (3) _____ of the senators are elected every (4) _____ year. To qualify for the office, a senator must be at least (5) _____ years of age, a U.S. citizen for at least (6)_____ years, and be a (7) _____ of the state which he or she was elected to represent. The president of the Senate is the (8) _____, who can only vote to (9) _____. When the vice president is absent, the (10) _____ directs Senate business. Being a senator and unlike the vice president, the president pro tempore can vote on any Senate issue. Finally, the Senate sits as a court and tries (11) _____. A (12) _____ vote is needed to convict and remove an official.

NOTES:
Look at the crossed-out portion in Section 3, clause 1. Since the adoption of Amendment 17 in 1913, Senators have been directly elected by the people instead of indirectly chosen by state legislatures. Amendment 17 also changed the vacancy rules as shown in clause 2. Like representatives (Section 2, clause 4), when a senator dies, resigns, or is removed from office, the state's governor holds an election to fill the vacancy. In addition, Amendment 17 allows state legislatures the right to give their state governor the power to appoint a temporary senator until the election is held.

Vocabulary Matching

Match the words in bold on this page to their definitions below by placing the word's number in the correct space as shown in the first example.

A. __16__ agreement, permission
B. _____ make
C. _____ "no" votes
D. _____ name, determine
E. _____ legal business
F. _____ meet
G. _____ given the power
H. _____ change
I. _____ minimum number to do law-making business
J. _____ meeting
K. _____ a number greater than half the total
L. _____ "yes" votes
M. _____ described by rules
N. _____ encourage or force
O. _____ rules
P. _____ retire, recess

Section 4

(1.) The times, places and manner of holding elections for senators and representatives, shall be **prescribed**[1] in each state by the legislature thereof; but the Congress may at any time by law make or **alter**[2] such **regulations**[3], except as to the places of choosing senators.

(2.) The Congress shall **assemble**[4] at least once in every year, ~~and such meeting shall be on the first Monday in December~~, unless they shall by law **appoint**[5] a different day.

Section 5

(1.) Each house shall be the judge of the elections, returns and qualifications of its own members, and a **majority**[6] of each shall **constitute**[7] a **quorum**[8] to do business; but a smaller number may **adjourn**[9] from day to day, and may be **authorized**[10] to **compel**[11] the attendance of absent members, in such manner, and under such penalties as each house may provide.

(2.) Each house may determine the rules of its **proceedings**[12], punish its members for disorderly behavior, and, with the concurrence of two-thirds, expel a member.

(3.) Each house shall keep a journal of its proceedings, and from time to time publish the same, excepting such parts as may in their judgment require secrecy; and the **yeas**[13] and **nays**[14] of the members of either house on any question shall, at the desire of one-fifth of those present, be entered on the journal.

(4.) Neither house, during the **session**[15] of Congress, shall, without the **consent**[16] of the other, adjourn for more than three days, nor to any other place than that in which the two houses shall be sitting.

NOTES:
The crossed-out portion in Section 4, clause 2 was changed by Amendment 20. Congress's session now begins January 3.

Know the Facts

Based on information from Article I, Sections 4 and 5, each of the following sentences is either true or false. Place a (+) in the space next to those sentences that are true and a (0) next to those sentences that are false. False sentences need to be corrected into true sentences as shown in the first example.

__0__ 1. Congress can decide not to meet each year.

   Congress must meet at least once a year.

_____ 2. Only a few members of Congress need to meet to make laws.

_____ 3. Congress has the power to change state congressmen election laws.

_____ 4. Three fifths of a house can approve to record a vote in their journal.

_____ 5. Congress can decide on what day of the year it will meet.

_____ 6. Congress decides how, when, and where elections are held for congressmen.

_____ 7. A three-fourths vote is needed to permanently remove a fellow member from either house.

_____ 8. Congress must always meet in the same place.

Section 6

(1.) The senators and representatives shall receive a **compensation**[1] for their services, to be **ascertained**[2] by law, and paid out of the treasury of the United States. They shall in all cases, except **treason**[3], **felony**[4] and **breach**[5] of the peace, be **privileged**[6] from arrest during their attendance at the session of their **respective**[7] houses, and in going to and returning from the same; and for any speech or debate in either house, they shall not be questioned in any other place.

Historical Background
To prevent abuses such as those in the past when a king would unjustly arrest members of Parliament to keep them from voting, the Constitution makes congressmen immune to arrest for less serious crimes (civil offenses, e.g., failure to pay debt) while carrying out legislative business.

(2.) No senator or representative shall, during the time for which he was elected, be appointed to any **civil**[8] office under the authority of the United States, which shall have been created, or the **emoluments**[9] **whereof**[10] shall have been increased during such time; and no person holding any office under the United States, shall be a member of either house during his continuance in office.

Section 7

(1.) All **bills**[11] for raising **revenue**[12] shall **originate**[13] in the House of Representatives; but the Senate may propose or **concur**[14] with amendments as on other bills.

(2.) Every bill which shall have passed the House of Representatives and the Senate, shall, before it become a law, be presented to the President of the United States; if he approve he shall sign it, but if not he shall return it, with his objections to that house in which it shall have originated, who shall enter the objections at large on their journal, and **proceed**[15] to **reconsider**[16] it. If after such reconsideration two-thirds of that house shall agree to pass the bill, it shall be sent, together with the objections, to the other house, by which it shall likewise be reconsidered, and if approved by two-thirds of that house, it shall become a law. But in all such cases the votes of both houses shall be determined by yeas and nays, and the names of the persons voting for and against the bill shall be entered on the journal of each house respectively. If any bill shall not be returned by the President within ten days, (Sundays **excepted**[17]) after it shall have been presented to him, the same shall be a law, in like manner as if he had signed it, unless the Congress by their adjournment prevent its return, in which case it shall not be a law.

(3.) Every order, **resolution**[18], or vote to which the concurrence of the Senate and House of Representatives may be necessary (except on a question of adjournment) shall be presented to the President of the United States; and before the same shall take effect, shall be approved by him, or being disapproved by him, shall be repassed by two-thirds of the Senate and House of Representatives, according to the rules and limitations prescribed in the case of a bill.

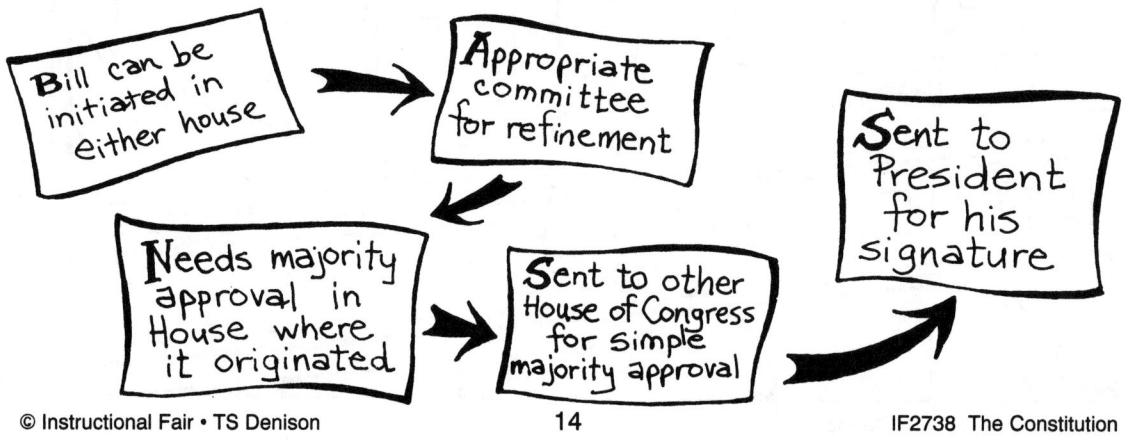

Bill can be initiated in either house → Appropriate committee for refinement → Needs majority approval in House where it originated → Sent to other House of Congress for simple majority approval → Sent to President for his signature

VOCABULARY MATCHING

Look at Article I, Sections 6 and 7 for the words in bold with numbers next to them. Match each word in bold to its definition below by placing the word's number in the correct space as shown in the first example.

A. __4__ serious crime (murder)
B. _____ immune
C. _____ payment and benefits
D. _____ laws passed to handle short-term, ceremonial, or unusual business
E. _____ a U.S. citizen helping (or becoming) an enemy of the United States
F. _____ community
G. _____ go forward
H. _____ money
I. _____ think over, reexamine
J. _____ break
K. _____ in regard to each
L. _____ of which
M. _____ determined
N. _____ earnings, wage
O. _____ agree
P. _____ begin
Q. _____ not included
R. _____ proposed laws

Know the Facts

Read both clauses of Section 6 and place a (P) next to statements that give congressmen privileges and (L) next to statements that limit the powers of congressmen.

1. _____ If the pay rate of a government job were increased during a congressman's current term, he or she could not be appointed to that job. This prevents misuse of power.

2. _____ Congressmen are to be paid for their service.

3. _____ Congressmen cannot be arrested for less serious crimes while performing their duties during meetings of the legislature.

4. _____ A congressman cannot be chosen for a government job which was created during his or her current term. This prevents conflicts of interest, a situation in which a person uses his or her position and power to improperly benefit him or herself. In an effort to promote the separation of each branch's powers and further avoid conflicts of interest, Section 6, clause 2 also makes it illegal for other government officials (e.g., the president or federal judges) to hold office as a congressman.

Resolutions Explained

Section 7, clauses 1 and 2 explain how bills become laws and are discussed in further detail on the following page. Clause 3 mentions a different type of legislation known as a *resolution*. There are three general types:

1) *Concurrent Resolutions* are passed by both houses to make rules that affect Congress (e.g., time of adjournment) or to express a joint opinion on some issue (e.g., voicing disapproval as the United States of another country's actions).

2) *Joint Resolutions* are like bills but deal with a limited issue (e.g., an emergency appropriation) or are used to propose amendments to the Constitution.

3) *Simple Resolutions* are proposed by one house to change its rules or express the feelings of Congress on an issue. Resolutions of this type do not require the other house's approval.

Concurrent and Simple Resolutions have no force as law and, therefore, do not require the president's signature for approval.

How a Bill Becomes a Law

Look back at Section 7, clauses 1 and 2 where the basics of how bills become laws are explained. Like much of the Constitution, the rules are worded in general terms as the framers intended, allowing for, as in this case, the first Congress and succeeding Congresses to make more detailed rules as needed. Below are seven paragraphs that briefly describe the steps required for a bill to become a law. However, the paragraphs are out of order and need to be numbered to show their correct order. The first paragraph is done for you as step number 6.

A. __6__ When both houses of Congress approve an identical version of the bill, the bill is sent to the president who can veto (reject) the bill or sign the bill into law. Not counting Sundays, the unsigned bill becomes law in ten days. However, the unsigned bill will not become law if Congress adjourns within the ten days and fails to receive the returned bill.

B. _____ A bill is introduced by a senator or representative in his or her respective house, but all bills to raise money must start in the House of Representatives. The clerk of the House or Senate "first reads" the bill (although the bill is not actually read) by attaching it with a title and number and then referring the bill to an appropriate committee.

C. _____ Congress can overturn a president's veto and make the bill a law with a two-thirds majority vote in both houses.

D. _____ Once assigned to a committee and possibly to a subcommittee by the full committee, the bill is debated in either committee (subcommittee first) by members who hold hearings to receive opinions and facts from members, experts, lobbyists, and citizens. The bill passes out of the subcommittee, possibly with changes if amendments were approved, and then it passes out of the full committee, if a majority of members from each committee approves.

E. _____ The bill is "third read" when the short title of the bill is read aloud and a roll-call vote is taken. The bill passes out of a house when a majority of the members present approve. The bill is then sent to the other house where steps 1-3 are repeated.

F. _____ "Second reading" of the bill occurs when the clerk receives the bill passed out of full committee. It is then sent to the floor of a house, where all members meet, debate, and possibly propose changes to the bill through amendments.

G. _____ In situations when the other house passes a different version of the bill it originally received (usually because of an amendment adopted at some point in the process), members of both houses meet as a conference committee to work out any disagreements between both versions of the bill. If a compromise is reached, the floors of both houses vote to approve an identical version of the bill by a majority vote.

THE POWERS OF CONGRESS

Fill in the missing letters for the words that help describe the powers of Congress. Powers 1-4 are described in Sections 1-3 and 7. Power 5 is described in Article II. However, most of Congress' powers (6-20) are listed in Section 8 as shown on the next page. Before looking at Section 8, try to figure out the missing letters within the parentheses as shown in question 1.

1. Make (L **A** **W** S)
2. (IN _ _ _ _ IGATE)—look into wrongdoing
3. (IM _ _ _ _ _ _)—remove officials
4. Overturns—(_ _ TOES)
5. Approve (T _ _ _ TIES), appointments
6. Borrow, Create (M _ _ _ _)
7. (_ _ X)—this is what the government uses to pays for things, e.g., roads
8. Make (T _ _ _ _ _) laws
9. Design U.S. (_ _ _ _ ZEN) rules
10. Define (BAN _ _ _ _ _ _ CY) laws
11. Fix (_ _ _ GHTS), measures
12. Define (FEL _ _ _) punishments
13. Create (_ _ _ _) offices
14. Promote (SC _ _ _ _ CE), (A _ _ S)
15. Protect (_ _ _ _ RIGHTS), patents
16. Establish federal (C _ _ _ _ _ S)
17. Declare (_ _ _)
18. Raise, regulate (_ _ _ ED) forces
19. Call for (M _ _ _ _ TIAS)
20. Maintain federal (L _ _ _ _)

Section 8

(1.) The Congress shall have power:
To **lay**[1] and collect taxes, duties, **imposts**[2] and **excises**[3], to pay the **debts**[4] and provide for the common defense and general welfare of the United States; but all duties, imposts and excises shall be **uniform**[5] throughout the United States;

(2.) To borrow money on the **credit**[6] of the United States;

(3.) To **regulate**[7] **commerce**[8] with foreign nations, and among the several states, and with the Indian tribes;

(4.) To **establish**[9] an uniform rule of **naturalization**[10], and uniform laws on the subject of **bankruptcies**[11] throughout the United States;

(5.) To coin money, regulate the value thereof, and of foreign coin, and **fix**[12] the standard of weights and measures;

(6.) To provide for the punishment of **counterfeiting**[13] the **securities**[14] and current coin of the United States;

(7.) To establish post offices and post roads;

(8.) To promote the progress of science and useful arts, by securing for limited times to authors and inventors the **exclusive**[15] right to their respective writings and discoveries;

(9.) To **constitute**[16] **tribunals**[17] **inferior**[18] to the Supreme Court;

(10.) To define and punish piracies and felonies committed on the high seas, and offenses against the law of nations;

(11.) To declare war, grant letters of **marque and reprisal**[19], and make rules concerning captures on land and water;

(12.) To **raise**[20] and support armies, but no **appropriation**[21] of money to that use shall be for a longer term than two years;

(13.) To provide and **maintain**[22] a navy;

(14.) To make rules for the government and regulation of the land and naval forces;

(15.) To provide for calling forth the **militia**[23] to **execute**[24] the laws of the Union, **suppress insurrections**[25] and **repel**[26] invasions;

(16.) To provide for organizing, arming, and disciplining, the militia, and for governing such part of them as may be employed in the service of the United States, reserving to the states respectively, the appointment of the officers, and the authority of training the militia according to the discipline prescribed by Congress;

(17.) To exercise exclusive legislation in all cases whatsoever, over such **district**[27] (not exceeding ten miles square) as may, by **cession**[28] of particular states, and the acceptance of Congress, become the seat of the government of the United States, and to exercise like authority over all places purchased by the consent of the legislature of the state in which the same shall be for the **erection**[29] of forts, **magazines**[30], arsenals, dockyards, and other needful buildings;— And

(18.) To make all laws which shall be necessary and proper for carrying into execution the foregoing powers, and all other powers vested by this Constitution in the government of the United States, or in any department or officer thereof.

Three Powers of Congress Explained

Section 8 lists most of Congress' powers. Clauses 1, 11, and 18 contain three of Congress' most important powers: the power to tax, to declare war, and to make all laws that are necessary and proper.

Clause 1: Under the Articles of Confederation, the Confederate Congress had no taxation power and, therefore, relied on the states for funds, funds which never were received. The framers of the U.S. Constitution corrected this problem, realizing that a strong central government must be able to raise money through taxes to pay expenses needed to carry out its duties and powers.

Clause 11: Only Congress can officially declare war. The framers wanted this power in the hands of many and not, as in the past, left up to one person, such as a king.

Clause 18: Since the Constitution was designed to be the basic blueprint for our government, the framers did not want and could not make rules covering every situation. For example, clause 13 requires Congress to provide for a Navy but does not say how it should be done. Therefore, they included the Necessary and Proper Clause, or Elastic Clause to provide Congress with the flexibility and power to pass any laws that were needed to carry out its duties and pass laws needed by the executive and judicial branches to carry out their Constitutional duties.

VOCABULARY MATCHING

PART I
Look in Section 8 for the words numbered 1-15 in bold. Match each word in bold to its definition below by placing the word's number in the correct space as shown in the first example.

A. _15_ sole
B. ____ making fake
C. ____ companies and people who cannot pay bills claim these
D. ____ create
E. ____ make rules for
F. ____ the same
G. ____ tax on goods made, sold, or used in the United States (tobacco)
H. ____ make
I. ____ taxes on imports
J. ____ bonds, stocks
K. ____ set
L. ____ granting citizenship
M. ____ trade between countries
N. ____ bank account, trust
O. ____ bills, money owed

PART II
Now look in Section 8 for the words numbered 16-30.

A. ____ support
B. ____ courts of justice
C. ____ decision to spend
D. ____ lower in order
E. ____ military supply warehouse
F. ____ to give up
G. ____ to defeat rebellions
H. ____ government land area
I. ____ defeat
J. ____ set up
K. ____ permission for private boat owners to capture or destroy enemy ships at war with United States
L. ____ build
M. ____ citizen/state army (National Guard)
N. ____ construction
O. ____ carry out

Section 9

*(1.) The **migration**[1] or **importation**[2] of such persons as any of the states now existing shall think proper to admit, shall not be **prohibited**[3] by the Congress prior to the year one thousand eight hundred and eight, but a tax or duty may be imposed on such importation, not exceeding ten dollars for each person.*

(2.) The privilege of the **writ of habeas corpus**[4] shall not be **suspended**[5], unless when in cases of rebellion or invasion the public safety may require it.

(3.) No **bill of attainder**[6] or **ex post facto law**[7] shall be passed.

(4.) No **capitation**[8], ~~or other direct,~~ tax shall be laid, unless in proportion to the **census**[9] or enumeration herein before directed to be taken.

(5.) No tax or duty shall be laid on **articles**[10] **exported**[11] from any state.

(6.) No **preference**[12] shall be given by any regulation of commerce or revenue to the ports of one state over those of another: nor shall vessels bound to, or from, one state, be **obliged**[13] to enter, clear, or pay duties in another.

(7.) No money shall be drawn from the **treasury**[14], but in consequence of appropriations made by law; and a regular statement and account of the receipts and **expenditures**[15] of all public money shall be published from time to time.

(8.) No title of **nobility**[16] shall be granted by the United States: And no person holding any office of profit or trust under them, shall, without the consent of the Congress, accept of any present, emolument, office, or title, of any kind whatever, from any king, prince, or **foreign state**[17].

VOCABULARY MATCHING

Look at Article I, Section 9 for the words in bold with numbers next to them. Match each word in bold to its definition below by placing the word's number in the correct space as shown in the first example.

A. __7__ a law that punishes the accused for something done before the law was passed
B. _____ delayed, ended
C. _____ a tax charged on each person in a population
D. _____ forbidden
E. _____ sold to another country
F. _____ people moving into the country
G. _____ requested
H. _____ another country
I. _____ spending
J. _____ a law that punishes a group or person without a trial
K. _____ a legal paper requiring a jailed person be charged with a crime or be released
L. _____ brought into a country
M. _____ count of population
N. _____ advantage, special treatment
O. _____ goods
P. _____ bank
Q. _____ a rank given by monarchs that raises a person above other citizens

Know the Facts

Read the following explanation of powers denied to Congress and match each description to its constitutional clause from Article I, Section 9. The first example is completed for you below.

A. __6__ Congress must pass laws that treat state ports equally, without preference given to one port over another. The provision also prevents Congress from passing laws which favor or discriminate one state's trade over others.

B. _____ Until Amendment 16, Congress could not tax incomes.

C. _____ Public records must be kept when Congress spends money. Money can only be spent by the government for purposes and amounts approved by Congress. This "power of the purse" allows Congress to check the powers of other branches.

D. _____ Congress cannot pass a law that allows the accused to be jailed indefinitely without being charged with a crime.

E. _____ This clause upholds the founders' belief that no one should receive special rights or privileges, that "all men are created equal." This provision also attempts to prevent bribes and corruption from foreign governments.

F. _____ Although outdated today, this clause allowed Congress to outlaw the slave trade in 1808. To prevent the Southern delegates from leaving the Constitutional Convention, this provision was included as part of the Slave Compromise.

G. _____ In an effort to promote trade and capitalism, Congress cannot tax goods manufactured in a state and sold to another country.

H. _____ Congress cannot pass a law which punishes a group or person without a trial or which punishes the accused for a crime committed before the law was passed. The framers wanted to prevent abuses committed by governments in the past.

Section 10

(1.) No state shall enter into any **treaty**[1], **alliance**[2], or **confederation**[3]; grant letters of marque and reprisal; coin money; **emit**[4] bills of credit; make anything but gold and silver coin a tender in payment of debts; pass any bill of attainder, *ex post facto* law, or law **impairing**[5] the **obligation**[6] of **contracts**[7], or grant any title of nobility.

(2.) No state shall, without the consent of the Congress, lay any imposts or duties on imports or exports, except what may be absolutely necessary for executing its inspection laws: and the **net**[8] produce of all duties and imposts, laid by any state on imports or exports, shall be for the use of the treasury of the United States; and all such laws shall be subject to the **revision**[9] and control of the Congress.

(3.) No state shall, without the consent of Congress, lay any duty of **tonnage**[10], keep troops, or ships of war in time of peace, enter into any agreement or **compact**[11] with another state, or with a foreign power, or engage in war, unless actually invaded, or in such **imminent**[12] danger as will not admit of delay.

Vocabulary Matching

Match each word in bold above to its definition below by placing the word's number in the correct space as shown in the first example.

A. __11__ alliance
B. _____ duty, requirements
C. _____ immediate
D. _____ a form of government in which independent states grant limited power to the central government
E. _____ agreements between countries/states
F. _____ legal agreements
G. _____ damaging, hindering
H. _____ partnership/pact between countries/states
I. _____ a vessel's cargo capacity
J. _____ change
K. _____ issue, release
L. _____ amount remaining after deductions

Know the Facts

Look at Article I, Section 10, clause 1, and list the nine restrictions on states as shown in the first example.

1. Make __treaties__
2. Make _____
3. Make _____
4. Make _____
5. Grant _____
6. Grant _____
7. Pass _____
8. Pass _____
9. Pass _____

NOTE: Unless they get permission from Congress, clauses 2 and 3 prevent the states from taxing trade and cargo capacity, keeping troops and ships of war during peace time, and making agreements with a foreign country or another state.

WHAT STATES CANNOT DO

Article II
Section 1

(1.) The executive power shall be vested in a President of the United States of America. He shall hold his office during the term of four years, and, together with the Vice-President, chosen for the same term, be elected, as follows:

(2.) Each state shall appoint, in such manner as the legislature thereof may direct, a number of electors, equal to the whole number of senators and representatives to which the state may be entitled in the Congress: but no senator or representative, or person holding an office of trust or profit under the United States, shall be appointed an elector.

> **Historical Background**
> The United States is the first country in history to create the office of president. The presidency is a position indirectly chosen by the people through electors from each state and is not granted based on birthright, such as when a prince becomes king when his father dies.

(3.) ~~The electors shall meet in their respective states, and vote by ballot for two persons, of whom one at least shall not be an inhabitant of the same state with themselves. And they shall make a list of all the persons voted for, and of the number of votes for each; which list they shall sign and certify, and transmit sealed to the seat of the government of the United States, directed to the president of the Senate. The president of the Senate shall, in the presence of the Senate and House of Representatives, open all the certificates, and the votes shall then be counted. The person having the greatest number of votes shall be the President, if such number be a majority of the whole number of electors appointed; and if there be more than one who have such majority, and have an equal number of votes, then the House of Representatives shall immediately choose by ballot one of them for President; and if no person have a majority, then from the five highest on the list the said House shall in like manner choose the President. But in choosing the President, the votes shall be taken by states, the representation from each state having one vote; a quorum for this purpose shall consist of a member or members from two thirds of the states, and a majority of all the states shall be necessary to a choice. In every case, after the choice of the President, the person having the greatest number of votes of the electors shall be the Vice President. But if there should remain two or more who have equal votes, the Senate shall choose from them by ballot the Vice President.~~

(4.) The Congress may determine the time of choosing the electors, and the day on which they shall give their votes; which day shall be the same throughout the United States.

(5.) No person except a natural-born citizen, or a citizen of the United States at the time of the adoption of this Constitution, shall be eligible to the office of President; neither shall any person be eligible to that office who shall not have attained to the age of thirty-five years, and been fourteen years a resident within the United States.

(6.) In case of the removal of the President from office, or of his death, resignation, or inability to discharge the powers and duties of the said office, the same shall devolve on the Vice-President, and the Congress may by law provide for the case of removal, death, resignation or inability, both of the President and Vice-President, declaring what officer shall then act as President, and such officer shall act accordingly, until the disability be removed, or a President shall be elected.

(7.) The President shall, at stated times, receive for his services, a compensation, which shall neither be increased nor diminished during the period for which he shall have been elected, and he shall not receive within that period any other emolument from the United States, or any of them.

(8.) Before he enter on the execution of his office, he shall take the following oath or affirmation:—"I do solemnly swear (or affirm) that I will faithfully execute the Office of President of the United States, and will to the best of my Ability, preserve, protect and defend the Constitution of the United States."

Know the Facts

Answer the following questions based on Article 2, Section 1 as shown in the first example.

1. What is the length of a president's term? _____4 years_____

2. Can a senator or representative be an elector? _____

3. During an election, who casts votes to determine the next president and vice president? (See Amendment 12 for more details.) _____

4. The president has to be a natural-born _____ and be at least how old? _____ and have lived in the United States for the last how many years? _____

5. Although elaborated on by Amendment 25, who performs the duties of president if the elected president dies? _____

Powers of the President

Look at Sections 1-4 of Article II and unscramble the following list of presidential powers as shown in the first example.

1. The HCFIE CUTEXEIVE _____Chief Executive_____ has the power to enforce and execute all laws.

2. The MOCNAMRED NI FHEIC _____ leads all military forces.

3. The president can KEPE VISROSDA _____ such as a Cabinet for counsel.

4. The president can NRATG ARDPNOS, PEVERISRE _____, meaning to forgive crimes.

5. The president can KEAM REATTSIE, PIONPTNEMTAS _____. Two thirds of the Senate must approve when these two powers are exercised. Except for federal judges, the first Congress also allowed the president the power to remove/dismiss appointments.

6. The president can CEMNMDOER SALW _____ and he can also veto proposed laws.

7. The president is AHDE FO ESATT _____ (receives diplomats, ambassadors, and other ministers).

NOTE: Section 1, clause 3 is no longer valid because of Amendment 12.

Section 2

(1.) The President shall be commander in chief of the Army and Navy of the United States, and of the militia of the several states, when called into the actual service of the United States; he may require the opinion, in writing, of the principal officer in each of the executive departments, upon any subject relating to the duties of their respective offices, and he shall have power to grant **reprieves**[1] and **pardons**[2] for offenses against the United States, except in cases of impeachment.

(2.) He shall have power, by and with the advice and consent of the Senate, to make treaties, provided two-thirds of the senators present concur; and he shall nominate, and by and with the advice and consent of the Senate, shall appoint ambassadors, other public ministers and consuls, judges of the Supreme Court, and all other officers of the United States, whose appointments are not herein otherwise provided for, and which shall be established by law: but the Congress may by law vest the appointment of such inferior officers, as they think proper, in the President alone, in the courts of law, or in the heads of departments.

(3.) The President shall have power to fill up all vacancies that may happen during the recess of the Senate, by granting **commissions**[3] which shall expire at the end of their next session.

Section 3

He shall from time to time give to the Congress information of the state of the Union, and recommend to their consideration such **measures**[4] as he shall judge necessary and **expedient**[5]; he may, on **extraordinary**[6] occasions, **convene**[7] both houses, or either of them, and in case of disagreement between them, with respect to the time of adjournment, he may adjourn them to such time as he shall think proper; he shall receive ambassadors and other public ministers; he shall take care that the laws be faithfully executed, and shall commission all the officers of the United States.

Section 4

The President, Vice-President, and all civil officers of the United States, shall be removed from office on impeachment for, and conviction of, treason, bribery, or other high crimes and **misdemeanors**[8].

VOCABULARY MATCHING

Match each word to the left in bold to its definition below by placing the word's number in the correct space as shown in the first example.

A. __5__ useful
B. _____ power given to a person to fulfill some duty or job
C. _____ postponement of sentence
D. _____ call together
E. _____ laws
F. _____ to release from punishment of a crime
G. _____ lesser crimes than felonies
H. _____ unusual, special

Article III
Section 1
The **judicial**[1] power of the United States, shall be vested in one Supreme Court, and in such inferior courts as the Congress may from time to time **ordain**[2] and establish. The judges, both of the Supreme and inferior courts, shall hold their offices during good behavior, and shall, at stated times, receive for their services, a compensation, which shall not be diminished during their continuance in office.

Section 2
(1.) The judicial power shall extend to all cases, in **law**[3] and **equity**[4], arising under this Constitution, the laws of the United States, and treaties made, or which shall be made, under their authority;—to all cases affecting ambassadors, other public ministers and consuls;—to all cases of **admiralty**[5] and **maritime**[6] **jurisdiction**[7];—to **controversies**[8] to which the United States shall be a **party**[9];—to controversies between two or more states; ~~between a state and citizens of another state~~; between citizens of different states;—between citizens of the same state claiming lands under grants of different states, and between a state, or the citizens thereof, and foreign states, citizens or **subjects**[10].

(2.) In all cases affecting ambassadors, other public ministers and consuls, and those in which a state shall be party, the Supreme Court shall have original jurisdiction. In all the other cases before mentioned, the Supreme Court shall have **appellate**[11] jurisdiction, both as to law and fact, with such exceptions, and under such regulations as the Congress shall make.

(3.) The trial of all crimes, except in cases of impeachment, shall be by jury; and such trial shall be held in the state where the said crimes shall have been committed; but when not committed within any state, the trial shall be at such place or places as the Congress may by law have directed.

Section 3
(1.) Treason against the United States, shall consist only in levying war against them, or in adhering to their enemies, giving them aid and comfort. No person shall be convicted of treason unless on the **testimony**[12] of two witnesses to the same **overt**[13] act, or on confession in open court.

(2.) The Congress shall have power to declare the punishment of treason, but no attainder of treason shall work corruption of **blood**[14], or **forfeiture**[15] except during the life of the person **attainted**[16].

Historical Background

Under the Articles of Confederation, there was no national judiciary. Each of the 13 states interpreted and applied the laws without consistency, often ignoring one another's court decisions. To settle disputes between states and protect people's rights from abusive laws passed by the states and the new federal government, the framers created the third branch. The judiciary branch decides arguments about what our laws mean, how they are applied, and whether a law is constitutional (i.e., Does it violate the Constitution?). Thus, the United States has a dual court system made up of state courts and federal courts.

Vocabulary Matching

Look at Article III for the words in bold and match each number to the definitions below as shown in the first example.

A. __7__ power to try such a case
B. ____ evidence
C. ____ sea (shipping) affairs
D. ____ punished
E. ____ management of justice (through courts, judges)
F. ____ naval affairs
G. ____ loss of rights
H. ____ to review and decide a court decision
I. ____ questions, disputes
J. ____ cases seeking judgment based on fairness
K. ____ open
L. ____ involved in a lawsuit
M. ____ judged under common laws—laws which may only guarantee fairness in specific situations
N. ____ punishment of a convicted person's relatives
O. ____ decree (order)
P. ____ people controlled by a country

Know the Facts

Read Article III and answer the questions by filling in the blanks as shown in the first example.

1. What is the highest court in the nation created by the Constitution?

   The Supreme Court

2. Who has the power to make all other federal courts and decide the size of the Supreme Court?

   _____

3. To make federal judges independent from political pressure or popular pressure, how long are their terms? (In the past, English kings have had judges unfairly punish their enemies and reward their friends.)

   _____

4. Looking at Article II, who has the power to appoint federal judges? Who must approve and by what fraction?

   _____
   _____
   _____

5. Who has final say, appellate and original jurisdiction, when deciding questions of whether a law, treaty, or executive action violates the Constitution? (This is called the power of judicial review and did not come about until after the *Marbury* v. *Madison* case in 1803.)

   _____

6. What is guaranteed in all federal criminal trials?

   _____

7. What is the only crime defined in the Constitution?

   _____

NOTE: the crossed out portion in Article III, section 2, clause 1 was made invalid by Amendment 11.

THE UNITED STATES SYSTEM OF GOVERNMENT

FEDERALISM
After having experienced first hand the failures and problems with a confederate form of government in which independent states had granted limited power to the central government, the framers realized they needed a stronger central government but not so strong that it would erase state and local government identities or threaten individual rights and freedoms. To preserve an acceptable level of local governments' independence and people's liberty, the framers decided on a federal system of government, a system in which a constitution defines how governmental powers are shared and divided between a national government and state governments. Both governments pass laws that operate on the same people and territory at the same time. However, unlike a confederate government, the national or federal government is stronger in power than the state or local governments.

SEPARATION OF POWERS
The U.S. Constitution lists and divides the national government's powers, limits, and responsibilities among three independent but coequal branches: the Legislative (Article I), Executive (Article II), and Judicial (Article III). Each branch has its own job, but all three must work together to keep things running smoothly. Having just fought for independence from a government who gave too much power to one person, a king, the framers wanted to prevent one branch from having too much power through its system of checks and balances.

CHECKS AND BALANCES
The framers wanted to achieve a balance of power among the three branches. To prevent one branch from controlling the other two branches and the national government from abusing its power, each branch uses its own powers to check the actions and powers of the other two branches. Thus, the powers of one branch are checked/limited/restrained by the powers of the other two.

SEPARATING, CHECKING, AND BALANCING THE POWERS
Place each letter from the following powers in its correct column on the diagram which appears on the following page. Notice that the location of the space and the arrows indicates how each branch uses its powers to check another branch. So, the D (remove federal judges through impeachment) in column 1 is a legislative power that checks the power of the judicial branch.

A. Carry out, recommend, veto laws
B. Decides how to spend money
C. Declare law or treaty unconstitutional
D. Remove federal judges through impeachment
E. Appoint federal judges
F. Approve federal judge appointments
G. Remove president by way of impeachment
H. Declare executive action unconstitutional
I. Approve treaties, presidential appointments
J. Can remove own appointments
K. Overturn president's veto
L. Create lower federal courts
M. Interprets laws without executive approval
N. Grant pardons and reprieves
O. Declare war, create armed forces
P. Call special meetings of Congress

BALANCE OF POWERS

LEGISLATIVE OVER EXECUTIVE

_____
_____
_____
_____

EXECUTIVE OVER LEGISLATIVE

_____
_____

LEGISLATIVE OVER JUDICIAL

D
_____
_____
_____

EXECUTIVE OVER JUDICIAL

_____
_____

JUDICIAL OVER LEGISLATIVE

_____

JUDICIAL OVER EXECUTIVE

_____
_____

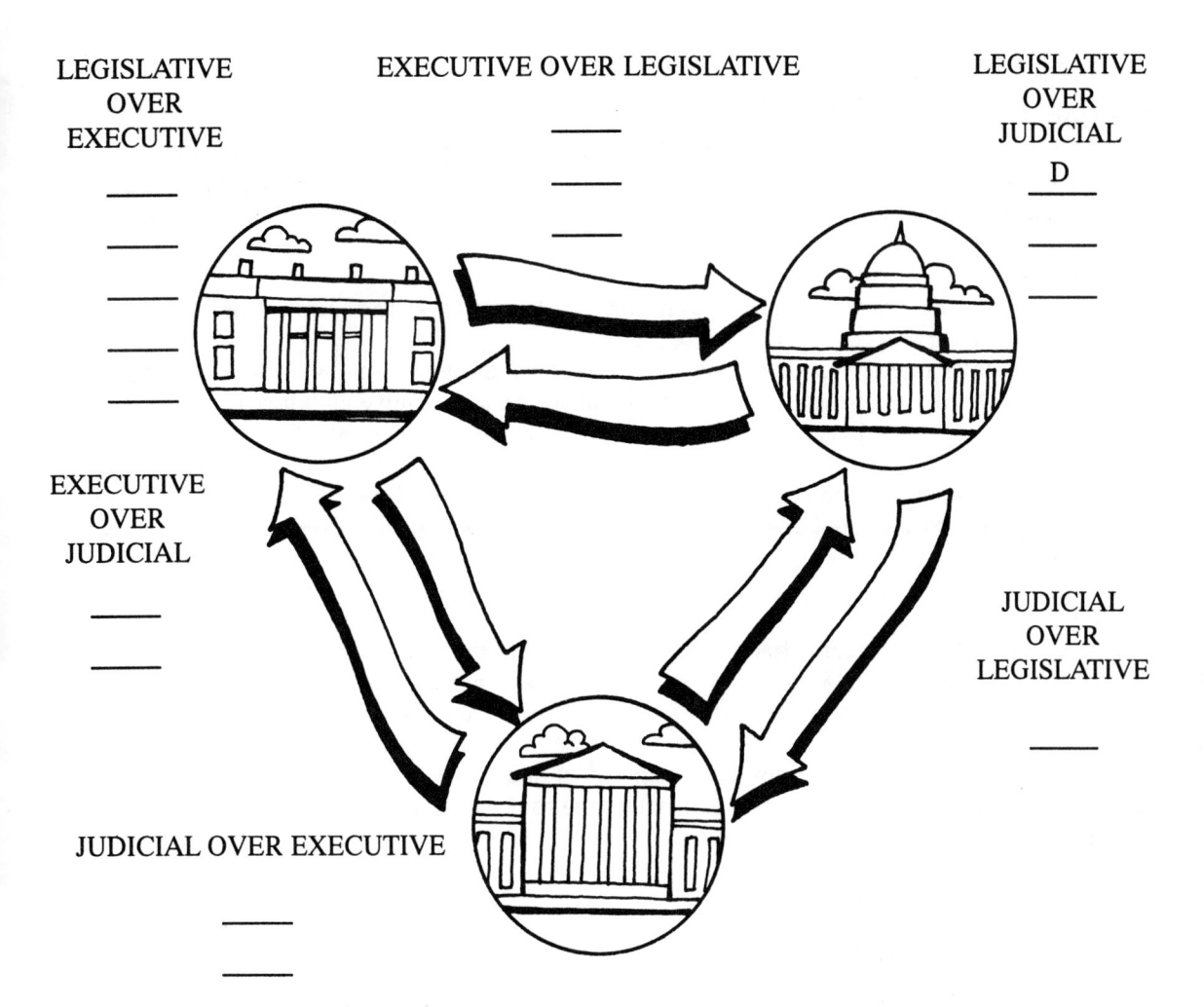

LIMITING THE POWERS
As provided in each article, the framers also wanted to limit the powers of each branch with term limits, requirements, and responsibilities. Place an (L), (E), or (J) next to each statement to indicate whether it is a Legislative (L), Executive (E), or Judicial (J) limit, responsibility, or requirement. Also write whether a legislative requirement is a Senate (S) or House of Representatives (R) limit as shown in the first example.

1. __L, S__ At least 30 years old
2. _____ At least 35 years old
3. _____ Settles arguments of law
4. _____ 2-year term, at least 1 per state
5. _____ 14-year resident in United States
6. _____ U.S. citizen for 7 years
7. _____ 6-year term, 2 per state

8. _____ 4-year term
9. _____ Makes laws
10. _____ Lifetime appointments
11. _____ U.S. citizen for 9 years
12. _____ Carries out laws
13. _____ Natural-born U.S. citizen
14. _____ At least 25 years old

Article IV
Section 1
Full faith and credit[1] shall be given in each state to the public acts, records, and judicial proceedings of every other state. And the Congress may by general laws prescribe the manner in which such acts, records and proceedings shall be proved, and the effect thereof.

Section 2
(1.) The citizens of each state shall be entitled to all **privileges**[2] and **immunities**[3] of citizens in the several states.

(2.) A person charged in any state with treason, felony, or other crime, who shall flee from justice, and be found in another state, shall on demand of the executive authority of the state from which he fled, be delivered up, to be removed to the state having jurisdiction of the crime.

(3.) ~~No person held to service or labor in one state, under the laws thereof, escaping into another, shall, in consequence of any law or regulation therein, be discharged from such service or labor, but shall be delivered up on claim of the party to whom such service or labor may be due~~.

Section 3
(1.) New states may be **admitted**[4] by the Congress into this Union; but no new state shall be formed or erected within the jurisdiction of any other state; nor any state be formed by the **junction**[5] of two or more states, or parts of states, without the consent of the legislatures of the states concerned as well as of the Congress.

(2.) The Congress shall have power to **dispose**[6] of and make all needful rules and regulations respecting the **territory**[7] or other property belonging to the United States; and nothing in this Constitution shall be so **construed**[8] as to **prejudice**[9] any claims of the United States, or of any particular state.

Section 4
The United States shall guarantee to every state in this Union a **republican**[10] form of government, and shall protect each of them against invasion; and on **application**[11] of the legislature, or of the executive (when the legislature cannot be convened) against domestic violence.

Vocabulary Matching

Look at Article IV for the words in bold and match each number to the definitions as shown in the first example.

A. __10__ a government run by representatives chosen by the people

B. _____ area of land

C. _____ written request

D. _____ allowed

E. _____ legal recognition

F. _____ bias, treat unfairly

G. _____ rights

H. _____ protections

I. _____ get rid

J. _____ understood

K. _____ joining

Know the Facts

Article IV deals with states' relations with one another and the federal government. Write answers in the spaces provided for each of the following questions as shown in the first example.

1. Who must recognize one another's legal decisions and records?

   _____the states_____

2. What is this recognition called?

   _____

3. Which clause says that a state cannot discriminate or treat unfairly citizens from other states?

   _____

4. What must a fugitive be charged with to be extradited (returned) to the state where the fugitive committed the crimes?

   _____, _____, and _____

5. Who has the power to demand the fugitive's return?

   _____

6. Although made invalid by Amendment 13, Section 2, clause 3 allowed owners the right to demand the return of their _____

7. Who has the power to admit new states into the Union and make rules on territories and property of the United States?

   _____

8. What type of government is promised to each state?

   _____

9. The federal government promises to protect the states against what two things?

   _____ and _____

Article V

The Congress, whenever two-thirds of both houses shall deem it necessary, shall **propose**[1] amendments to this Constitution, or, on the application of the legislatures of two-thirds of the several states, shall call a **convention**[2] for proposing amendments, which, in either case, shall be **valid**[3] to all intents and purposes, as part of this Constitution, when **ratified**[4] by the legislatures of three-fourths of the several states, or by conventions in three-fourths thereof, as the one or the other mode of ratification may be proposed by the Congress; provided ~~that no amendment which may be made prior to the year one thousand eight hundred and eight shall in any manner affect the first and fourth clauses in the ninth section of the first article; and~~ that no state, without its consent, shall be **deprived**[5] of its equal **suffrage**[6] in the Senate.

Article VI

(**1.**) All **debts**[7] contracted and engagements entered into, before the adoption of this Constitution, shall be as valid against the United States under this Constitution, as under the Confederation.

(**2.**) This Constitution, and the laws of the United States which shall be made in **pursuance**[8] thereof; and all treaties made, or which shall be made, under the authority of the United States, shall be the **supreme**[9] law of the land; and the judges in every state shall be bound thereby, anything in the constitution or laws of any state to the contrary notwithstanding.

(**3.**) The senators and representatives before mentioned, and the members of the several state legislatures, and all executive and judicial officers, both of the United States and of the several states, shall be bound by oath or affirmation, to support this Constitution; but no religious test shall ever be required as a qualification to any office or public trust under the United States.

Historical Background

The framers wanted a flexible constitution that could grow and change to meet future demands. Under the Articles of Confederation, all the states had to agree to any changes. The framers realized that it was too difficult to get everyone to agree unanimously, but they did not want to make it too easy either with just a majority vote. In terms of methods of proposing and approving amendments to the Constitution, all Amendment 21, were proposed by Congress and ratified by the states. Only Amendment 21 was proposed and ratified by the convention method. Amendments are proposed as joint resolutions and then, if passed by a two-thirds majority, they are sent to the states for consideration. The amendment process does not require a president's signature. NOTE: The crossed out portion was made invalid after 1808 when Congress was allowed to ban the slave trade, which they did.

Article VI, clause 1 is outdated since it was included to guarantee the states that the new federal government would honor the debts of the Confederate Congress.

Many people came to America to escape religious oppression by governments, like that of England, so the framers made certain there was a separation of church and state by not requiring a religious test. The first amendment would make this fact even clearer. Finally, Rhode Island never sent any delegates to the convention, which explains why only delegates from 12 states approved. Rhode Island did not want a stronger central government.

Article VII

The ratification of the conventions of nine states, shall be sufficient for the establishment of this Constitution between the states so ratifying the same.

Done in Convention by the **unanimous**[10] consent of the states present the seventeenth day of September in the year of our Lord one thousand seven hundred and eighty-seven and of the independence of the United States of America the twelfth. In witness whereof we have hereunto subscribed our names.

George Washington—President and Deputy from Virginia

NEW HAMPSHIRE	NEW JERSEY	DELAWARE	NORTH CAROLINA
John Langdon	William Livingston	George Read	William Blount
Nicholas Gilman	David Brearley	Gunning Bedford, Jr.	Richard Dobbs Spaight
	William Paterson	John Dickinson	Hugh Williamson
MASSACHUSETTS	Jonathan Dayton	Richard Bassett	
Nathaniel Gorham		Jacob Broom	SOUTH CAROLINA
Rufus King	PENNSYLVANIA		John Rutledge
	Benjamin Franklin	MARYLAND	Charles Cotesworth Pinckney
CONNECTICUT	Thomas Mifflin	James McHenry	Charles Pinckney
William Samuel Johnson	Robert Morris	Dan of St. Thomas Jenifer	Pierce Butler
Roger Sherman	George Clymer	Daniel Carroll	
	Thomas FitzSimons		GEORGIA
NEW YORK	Jared Ingersoll	VIRGINIA	William Few
Alexander Hamilton	James Wilson	John Blair	Abraham Baldwin
	Gouverneur Morris	James Madison, Jr.	

VOCABULARY MATCHING

Look at Articles V–VII for the words in bold and match each number to the definitions below as shown in the first example.

A. __9__ highest
B. _____ approved
C. _____ assembly
D. _____ bills, money owed
E. _____ present to decide
F. _____ kept from having
G. _____ all together
H. _____ vote
I. _____ legal
J. _____ accordance with

Know the Facts

Answer the questions in the spaces provided as shown in the first example.

1. What two methods can an amendment be proposed and by what fraction?
   __Congress__ , _____ , _____

2. Who ratifies/approves amendments and by what fraction? _____ , _____

3. No amendment can be passed that affects what?
   _____

4. What is the highest law of the land? _____
   All other laws (treaties, federal laws, state constitutions, state statutes, and city/town laws) must agree with the Constitution.

5. What cannot be required as a qualification to become a public official? _____

AMENDMENTS TO THE U.S. CONSTITUTION

Historical Background

The states approved the Constitution with the understanding that the first Congress would propose amendments guaranteeing the rights of individuals. Congress kept its promise and proposed 12 amendments from over 100 proposals that were submitted to Congress by the states. The original first amendment dealt with adjusting the ratio of representatives to population in Congress, but was never approved. It would take 203 years before the original second amendment was approved in 1992 as Amendment 27. Thus, the original third amendment became what is known today as the first amendment. All ten amendments were approved on September 25, 1789.

Except for Amendments 8 and 9, the Bill of Rights generally guarantees inalienable, individual rights of political participation and of the accused. This means that the right to free speech cannot be taken away because it is a basic human right. Until the twentieth century, the Bill of Rights limited federal actions and not the states' actions because many of the states' constitutions guaranteed the same rights. The states wanted to make certain that the new federal government would not restrict their rights. However, Amendment 14's due process clause has allowed twentieth-century Supreme Courts to rule that almost all of the Bill of Rights' provisions apply to the states as well. Read Amendment 14 for more detail.

Regarding the other 17 amendments, they either increased citizenship and voting rights or changed Congress, the presidency, and/or the courts. Just as the framers intended, all have been passed to help make an eighteenth-century document meet the needs of a nineteenth-, twentieth-, and hopefully a twenty-first-century United States.

AMENDMENT 1
Congress shall make no law respecting an establishment of religion, or prohibiting the free exercise thereof; or **abriding**[1] the freedom of speech, or of the press; or the right of the people peaceably to assemble, and to **petition**[2] the government for a **redress**[3] of **grievances**[4].

AMENDMENT 2
A well-regulated militia, being necessary to the security of a free state, the right of the people to keep and **bear**[5] arms shall not be **infringed**[6].

AMENDMENT 3
No soldier shall, in time of peace be **quartered**[7] in any house, without the consent of the owner, nor in time of war, but in a manner to be prescribed by law.

AMENDMENT 4
The right of the people to be secure in their persons, houses, papers, and effects, against unreasonable searches and seizures, shall not be violated, and no **warrants**[8] shall issue, but upon probable cause, supported by oath or affirmation, and particularly describing the place to be searched, and the persons or things to be **seized**[9].

Vocabulary Matching

Look at Amendments 1, 2, 3, and 4 for the words in bold and match each number to the definitions below as shown in the first example.

A. __9__ taken

B. _____ housed

C. _____ request

D. _____ correction

E. _____ carry

F. _____ wrongs

G. _____ reducing

H. _____ broken

I. _____ legal documents allowing some action

Know the Facts

Look at Amendments 1-4 and answer the following questions as shown in the first example.

1. List the first amendment's five guarantees:

    Freedom of religion
    _____
    _____
    _____
    _____

2. What does Amendment 2 guarantee?
    _____
    _____

3. What does Amendment 3 guarantee?
    _____
    _____

4. What does Amendment 4 guarantee? What is needed to do this?
    _____
    _____

AMENDMENT 5

No person shall be held to answer for a **capital**[1], or otherwise **infamous**[2] crime, unless on a **presentment**[3] or indictment of a grand jury, except in cases arising in the land or naval forces, or in the militia, when in actual service in time of war or public danger; nor shall any person be subject for the same offense to be twice put in **jeopardy**[4] of life or limb; nor shall be compelled in any criminal case to be a witness against himself, nor be deprived of life, liberty, or property, without **due process**[5] of law; nor shall private property be taken for public use, without just compensation.

AMENDMENT 6

In all criminal **prosecutions**[6], the accused shall enjoy the right to a speedy and public trial, by an **impartial**[7] jury of the state and district wherein the crime shall have been committed, which district shall have been previously ascertained by law, and to be informed of the nature and cause of the accusation; to be confronted with the witnesses against him; to have **compulsory**[8] process for obtaining witnesses in his favor, and to have the assistance of **counsel**[9] for his defense.

AMENDMENT 7

In **suits**[10] at common law, where the value in controversy shall exceed twenty dollars, the right of trial by jury shall be **preserved**[11], and no fact tried by a jury, shall be otherwise reexamined in any court of the United States, than according to the rules of the common law.

AMENDMENT 8

Excessive[12] **bail**[13] shall not be required, nor excessive **fines**[14] imposed, nor cruel and unusual punishments inflicted.

AMENDMENT 9

The enumeration in the Constitution, of certain rights, shall not be construed to **deny**[15] or **disparage**[16] others retained by the people.

AMENDMENT 10

The powers not **delegated**[17] to the United States by the Constitution, nor prohibited by it to the states, are **reserved**[18] to the states respectively, or to the people.

Vocabulary Matching

Look at Amendments 5–10 for the words in bold and match each number to the definitions below as shown in the first example.

A. __12__ unfair, unreasonable
B. _____ not recognize
C. _____ upheld, protected
D. _____ punishable by death
E. _____ presentation
F. _____ money penalty
G. _____ lawyer, legal advice
H. _____ on trial
I. _____ given
J. _____ widely known and terrible
K. _____ payment by the accused to be released from jail until the trial begins
L. _____ rules and laws through courts of justice that protect individual rights
M. _____ retained, set aside
N. _____ a legal action in which a party takes another to court
O. _____ order to have a witness appear in court for examination
P. _____ legal actions against a person
Q. _____ not biased
R. _____ reduce

Know the Facts

Look at Amendments 5–10 and match each description below to its correct amendment as shown in the first example. Some amendments will have more than one description match.

A. __9__ People have basic rights (e.g., freedom to travel) not listed in the Constitution.
B. _____ No person can be tried more than once for the same crime (i.e., no double jeopardy).
C. _____ Right to a speedy trial.
D. _____ Right of the accused to question witnesses testifying against him or her.
E. _____ Right to trial by jury in criminal cases.
F. _____ Protects from cruel and unusual punishment.
G. _____ The government must pay fair prices for land it needs.
H. _____ Right of the accused to urge witnesses to testify on their behalf.
I. _____ Right to know reason for arrest.
J. _____ The states and the people have powers not listed or forbidden in the Constitution (e.g., have public schools).
K. _____ Right to due process.
L. _____ Right to have a lawyer.
M. _____ Protects from unfair bails and high fines.
N. _____ Right to remain silent (plead the fifth).
O. _____ Right to trial by jury in civil/non-criminal cases.

AMENDMENT 11
The judicial power of the United States shall not be construed to extend to any suit in law or equity, **commenced**[1] or **prosecuted**[2] against one of the United States by citizens of another state, or by citizens or subjects of any foreign state.

AMENDMENT 12
The electors shall meet in their respective states and vote by **ballot**[3] for President and Vice-President, one of whom, at least, shall not be an inhabitant of the same state with themselves; they shall name in their ballots the person voted for as President, and in **distinct**[4] ballots the person voted for as Vice-President, and they shall make distinct lists of all persons voted for as President, and of all persons voted for as Vice-President, and of the number of votes for each, which lists they shall sign and **certify**[5], and **transmit**[6] sealed to the seat of the government of the United States, directed to the president of the Senate;—the President of the Senate shall, in the presence of the Senate and House of Representatives, open all the certificates and the votes shall then be counted;—the person having the greatest number of votes for President, shall be the President, if such number be a **majority**[7] of the whole number of electors appointed; and if no person have such majority, then from the persons having the highest numbers not exceeding three on the list of those voted for as President, the House of Representatives shall choose immediately, by ballot, the President. But in choosing the President, the votes shall be taken by states, the representation from each state having one vote; a quorum for this purpose shall consist of a member or members from two-thirds of the states, and a majority of all the states shall be necessary to a choice. And if the House of Representatives shall not choose a President whenever the right of choice shall devolve upon them, ~~before the fourth day of March next following~~, then the Vice-President shall act as President, as in the case of the death or other constitutional disability of the President.—The person having the greatest number of votes as Vice-President, shall be the Vice-President, if such number be a majority of the whole number of electors appointed, and if no person have a majority, then from the two highest numbers on the list, the Senate shall choose the Vice-President; a quorum for the purpose shall consist of two-thirds of the whole number of senators, and a majority of the whole number shall be necessary to a choice. But no person constitutionally **ineligible**[8] to the office of President shall be eligible to that of Vice-President of the United States.

Historical Background
Amendment 11 was approved on February 7, 1795, to relieve fears that the British would sue for Revolutionary War losses and that the states would lose their independence if the federal courts had original jurisdiction in suits from other state citizens. Amendment 13 was approved after the Civil War on December 6, 1865, to forever end the nearly 100-year slavery debate.

AMENDMENT 13
Section 1
Neither slavery nor **involuntary**[9] **servitude**[10], except as a punishment for crime whereof the party shall have been **duly**[11] convicted, shall exist within the United States, or any place subject to their jurisdiction.

Section 2
Congress shall have power to enforce this article by appropriate legislation.

VOCABULARY MATCHING

Look at Amendments 11, 12, and 13 for the words in bold and match each number to the definitions below as shown in the first example.

- A. __2__ brought before a court of law
- B. _____ separate, not identical
- C. _____ without choice, against one's will
- D. _____ a number greater than half the total
- E. _____ voting form
- F. _____ send
- G. _____ slavery
- H. _____ not allowed
- I. _____ confirm
- J. _____ started

Historical Background

Approved June 15, 1804, Amendment 12 replaced the original method for election of the president as outlined in Article II, Section 1, clause 3 because of what happened during the election of 1800. Before the election, political parties emerged (something the framers never envisioned would occur), and since there was an equal number of electors pledged to vote for their party, it took 36 ballots in the House of Representatives before Jefferson finally won the presidency. Under the present system, the people (previously the state legislators chose electors since most of the framers believed that the people were not capable enough to make the important decision) are not directly voting for a president, but for presidential electors.

Each state has a number of electors equal to its number of representatives and senators in Congress. Even though not a state, Washington, D.C., gets three electors because of Amendment 23. Thus, since there are 435 representatives, 100 senators, and three electors from Washington, D.C., there are a total of 538 electors. A candidate needs 270 to win the presidency. In fact, on election day in November, there are actually 51 separate elections for president by the people in each of the 50 states and Washington, D.C. The candidate with the most popular (people) votes in each state receives all of that state's electoral votes. So if a candidate won by a few thousand votes in California, that candidate would receive all 54 of California's electoral votes. In other words, winner takes all! Note: the crossed-out portion was changed by Amendment 20.

Know the Facts

Answer the following questions on Amendments 11, 12, and 13.

1. Under Amendment 11, what two groups cannot start suits against a state in federal court?

    _____

    _____

2. Which house makes the choice for president if there is no majority? _____ and for vice president if there is no majority? _____

3. Could a candidate become vice president if under 35 years old or foreign born? _____

4. What does Amendment 13 no longer allow? _____

AMENDMENT 14

Section 1

All persons born or naturalized in the United States, and subject to the jurisdiction thereof, are citizens of the United States and of the state wherein they reside. No state shall make or enforce any law which shall abridge the privileges or immunities of citizens of the United States; nor shall any state deprive any person of life, liberty, or property, without due process of law; nor deny to any person within its jurisdiction the equal protection of the laws.

Section 2

Representatives shall be apportioned among the several states according to their respective numbers, counting the whole number of persons in each state, ~~excluding Indians not taxed~~. *But when the right to vote at any election for the choice of electors for President and Vice-President of the United States, representatives in Congress, the executive and judicial officers of a state, or the members of the legislature thereof, is denied to any of the male inhabitants of such state, being twenty-one years of age, and citizens of the United States, or in any way abridged, except for participation in rebellion, or other crime, the basis of representation therein shall be reduced in the proportion which the number of such male citizens shall bear to the whole number of male citizens twenty-one years of age in such state.*

Section 3

No person shall be a senator or representative in Congress, or elector of President and Vice-President, or hold any office, civil or military, under the United States, or under any state, who, having previously taken an oath, as a member of Congress, or as an officer of the United States, or as a member of any state legislature, or as an executive or judicial officer of any state, to support the Constitution of the United States, shall have engaged in insurrection or rebellion against the same, or given aid or comfort to the enemies thereof. But Congress may by a vote of two-thirds of each House, remove such disability.

Section 4

The **validity**[1] of the public debt of the United States, authorized by law, including debts **incurred**[2] for payment of **pensions**[3] and **bounties**[4] for services in **suppressing**[5] insurrection or rebellion, shall not be questioned. But neither the United States nor any state shall assume or pay any debt or obligation incurred in aid of insurrection or rebellion against the United States, or any claim for the loss or **emancipation**[6] of any slave; but all such debts, obligations and claims shall be held illegal and void.

Section 5

The Congress shall have power to enforce, by appropriate legislation, the **provisions**[7] of this article.

Vocabulary Matching

Look at Amendment 14 for the words in bold and match each number to the definitions below as shown in the first example.

- A. __1__ legality, legitimacy
- B. _____ money benefits
- C. _____ earned, acquired
- D. _____ rewards
- E. _____ freeing
- F. _____ putting down
- G. _____ requirements, conditions

Know the Facts

Read Amendment 14 and fill in the blanks as shown in the first example.

1. Who can become U.S. citizens? _____ and _____

2. What is needed to deprive someone of life, freedom, and property? _____

3. What cannot be denied to a U.S. citizen? _____

Historical Background

Section 1 of Amendment 14 is one of the most important Constitutional provisions because it made former slaves citizens of the United States and prevented states from passing laws that denied citizens their equal rights.

With Amendment 1 beginning with "Congress shall make no law . . . ," for over a hundred years the Bill of Rights was interpreted to protect the states and state citizens from national government abuses; it did not protect citizens from state laws. However, even after Amendment 14 was approved on July 9, 1868, it was not until 1925 that the Supreme Court took the first step in applying the Bill of Rights to state actions through Amendment 14's due process clause: "[no]. . . state shall deprive any person of life, liberty, or property, without due process of law . . . ." Except for Amendments 2, 3, and 10 (which do not apply) and the guarantees of trial by jury in civil cases and trial by grand jury for serious crimes, the states, just like the federal government, must meet all of the Bill of Rights' requirements.

How the states must meet the requirements was further defined and upheld by the Supreme Court through Amendment 14's equal protection clause. Originally drafted to prevent the South from having laws that unfairly treated former slaves, this clause guarantees everyone equal protection under the law, regardless, for example, of race or gender.

The first sentence of Section 2 replaces Article 1, Section 2, clause 3 and ends the Slave Compromise of counting every slave as three fifths of a person. Instead, all people in each state are counted towards determining the number of representatives a state has in the House of Representatives. The rest of Section 2 is considered out-of-date when considering that Amendments 19 and 26 have opened up voting to women and those who are at least 18.

In 1898 two thirds of Congress removed Section 3's prevention on those who took an oath to support the Constitution and then fought the United States in a rebellion (the Civil War), from ever again holding a United States' office.

Section 4 prevented the former Confederate South from suing the federal government or the states to pay off losses incurred during the Civil War or because slaves were freed.

AMENDMENT 15
Section 1
The right of citizens of the United States to vote shall not be denied or abridged by the United States or by any state on account of race, color, or previous condition of servitude.

Section 2
The Congress shall have power to enforce this article by appropriate legislation.

AMENDMENT 16
The Congress shall have power to lay and collect taxes on incomes, from whatever source derived, without apportionment among the several states, and without regard to any census or enumeration.

AMENDMENT 17
Section 1
The Senate of the United States shall be composed of two senators from each state, elected by the people thereof for six years; and each senator shall have one vote. The electors in each state shall have the qualifications requisite for electors of the most numerous branch of the state legislatures.

Section 2
When vacancies happen in the representation of any state in the Senate, the executive authority of such state shall issue writs of election to fill such vacancies: Provided, That the legislature of any state may empower the executive thereof to make temporary appointments until the people fill the vacancies by election as the legislature may direct.

Section 3
This amendment shall not be so construed as to affect the election or term of any senator chosen before it becomes valid as part of the Constitution.

AMENDMENT 18
~~Section 1~~
~~After one year from the ratification of this article the manufacture, sale, or transportation of intoxicating liquors within, the importation thereof into, or the exportation thereof from the United States and all territory subject to the jurisdiction thereof for beverage purposes is hereby prohibited.~~

~~Section 2~~
~~The Congress and the several states shall have concurrent power to enforce this article by appropriate legislation.~~

~~Section 3~~
~~This article shall be inoperative unless it shall have been ratified as an amendment to the Constitution by the legislatures of the several states, as provided in the Constitution, within seven years from the date of the submission hereof to the states by the Congress.~~

Historical Background

Like Amendments 13 and 14, Amendment 15 was passed after the Civil War, approved on February 3, 1870, to prevent the defeated South from treating former slaves unfairly.

It was not until 43 years later that Amendment 16 was approved on February 25, 1913, to allow Congress to tax incomes without regard to state populations. A tax limited by population (as what was required by the Article I, Section 2, clause 3 and Section 9, clause 4) would have required a state with greater population to pay more taxes even if the state had less combined income than a state with fewer people. Thus, an income tax was considered fairer and more necessary to carry out the growing federal government's duties and responsibilities as demanded by twentieth century events, for example, World War I and II.

Amendment 17 was approved on May 31, 1913, after years of protest by laborers and farmers wanting to directly elect (vote for) senators who represented their views and ending election of senators by state legislatures as outlined in Article I, Section 3. In the later half of the nineteenth century, the Senate was generally believed to be corrupt and definitely often supported pro-business/anti-labor/anti-farmer legislation.

The only amendment to be later repealed, Amendment 18 was approved on January 16, 1919, in an effort to stop the making, selling, transporting, importing, or exporting of alcohol.

Know the Facts

Read Amendments 15-18 and fill in the blanks as shown in the first example.

1. A citizen can vote regardless of what three things?

   ____Race____, _____, _____

2. Congress can collect what on incomes? _____

3. What official is elected directly by the people? _____

4. What did Amendment 18 ban? _____

AMENDMENT 19
Section 1
The right of citizens of the United States to vote shall not be denied or abridged by the United States or by any state on account of sex.

Section 2
Congress shall have power to enforce this article by appropriate legislation.

AMENDMENT 20
Section 1
The terms of the President and Vice-President shall end at noon on the 20th day of January, and the terms of senators and representatives at noon on the third day of January, of the year in which such terms would have ended if this article had not been ratified; and the terms of their successors shall then begin.

Section 2
The Congress shall assemble at least once in every year, and such meeting shall begin at noon on the third day of January, unless they shall by law appoint a different day.

Section 3
If, at the time fixed for the beginning of the term of the President, the President elect shall have died, the Vice-President elect shall become President. If a President shall not have been chosen before the time fixed for the beginning of his term, or if the President elect shall have failed to qualify, then the Vice-President elect shall act as President until a President shall have qualified; and the Congress may by law provide for the case wherein neither a President elect nor a Vice-President elect shall have qualified, declaring who shall then act as President, or the manner in which one who is to act shall be selected, and such person shall act accordingly until a President or Vice-President shall have qualified.

Section 4
The Congress may by law provide for the case of the death of any of the persons from whom the House of Representatives may choose a President whenever the right of choice shall have devolved upon them, and for the case of the death of any of the persons from whom the Senate may choose a Vice-President whenever the right of choice shall have devolved upon them.

Section 5
Sections 1 and 2 shall take effect on the 15th day of October following the ratification of this article.

Section 6
This article shall be inoperative unless it shall have been ratified as an amendment to the Constitution by the legislatures of three-fourths of the several states within seven years from the date of its submission.

Historical Background

Before Amendment 19 was approved on August 26, 1920, western territories since 1869 (Wyoming being the first) had allowed women to vote in an effort to draw women to their territories. After many women worked in jobs traditionally held by men during World War I and Amendment 18 passed (the anti-liquor movement was led by many women and opposed by men who did not want to give women the vote because they might use their voting power to outlaw liquor), the long battle for equal suffrage based on gender was over.

On January 23, 1933, Amendment 20 changed the dates on which the president's and Congress' terms begin. Since elections take place in November, under the old dates, there was too much time between when an elected official would replace a defeated official. The time was shortened in an effort to prevent a defeated official, or "lame duck," from passing laws that his or her constituents would not approve. In other words, the official would not have to worry about doing something that might risk his or her reelection chances since the official has already been voted out of office! Amendment 20 also provides rules for if the president elect or vice president elect dies before taking office.

Know the Facts

Read Amendments 19 and 20 and fill in the blanks.

1. Amendment 19 prevents denying the right to vote based on what? _____

2. Who was able to vote after passage of Amendment 19? _____

3. When do the president's and vice president's terms end? _____

4. When does a term of Congress begin? _____

5. Why were sections 1 and 2 included in Amendment 20? _____

_____

6. Who becomes the president elect if the president elect dies? _____

AMENDMENT 21
Section 1
The eighteenth article of amendment to the Constitution of the United States is hereby repealed.

Section 2
The transportation or importation into any state, territory, or possession of the United States for delivery or use therein of intoxicating liquors, in violation of the laws thereof, is hereby prohibited.

Section 3
This article shall be inoperative unless it shall have been ratified as an amendment to the Constitution by conventions in the several states, as provided in the Constitution, within seven years from the date of the submission hereof to the states by the Congress.

AMENDMENT 22
Section 1
No person shall be elected to the office of the President more than twice, and no person who has held the office of President, or acted as President, for more than two years of a term to which some other person was elected President shall be elected to the office of the President more than once. But this article shall not apply to any person holding the office of President when this Article was proposed by the Congress, and shall not prevent any person who may be holding the office of President, or acting as President, during the term within which this article becomes operative from holding the office of President or acting as President during the remainder of such term.

Section 2
This article shall be inoperative unless it shall have been ratified as an amendment to the Constitution by the legislatures of three-fourths of the several states within seven years from the day of its submission to the states by the Congress.

AMENDMENT 23
Section 1
The district constituting the seat of government of the United States shall appoint in such manner as the Congress may direct: A number of electors of President and Vice-President equal to the whole number of senators and representatives in Congress to which the district would be entitled if it were a state, but in no event more than the least populous state; they shall be in addition to those appointed by the states, but they shall be considered, for the purposes of the election of President and Vice-President, to be electors appointed by a state; and they shall meet in the district and perform such duties as provided by the twelfth article of amendment.

Section 2
The Congress shall have power to enforce this article by appropriate legislation.

Historical Background

Amendment 21 became the first and only amendment to date which was ratified by the state convention method and also the only amendment to repeal (cancel) another amendment, Amendment 18. Efforts to reduce consumption of alcohol resulted in increased crime. In addition, two important events occurred before the amendment was approved on December 5, 1933: 1) the Great Depression had been raging since 1929 and many believed that legalization of alcohol could provide more money in taxes to the government and jobs to the unemployed, 2) The republicans who supported prohibition were voted out of office and replaced by democrats who promised to repeal Amendment 18.

Franklin D. Roosevelt was the first and only president to serve office more than two terms, breaking a two-term tradition set by previous presidents. He was on his fourth term and twelfth year in office before he died in 1945. Soon after Amendment 22 was approved on February 27, 1951, to prevent an imbalance of power held by a president continuing office beyond a second term. For example, being in office so long, Roosevelt nominated eight associate Supreme Court justices and one chief justice.

On March 29, 1961, Amendment 23 was approved granting voters in the District of Columbia the right to vote for presidential and vice presidential electors.

Know the Facts

Read Amendments 21, 22, and 23 and fill in the blanks.

1. Section 1 of Amendment 21 does what? _____

2. Who has the power to regulate the transportation or importation of alcohol? _____

3. How was Amendment 21 ratified? _____

4. According to Amendment 22, how many terms can a president serve? _____

5. What is the maximum number of years a vice president can be president if reelected after having replaced the former president? _____

6. If the least populous state in the Union has two senators and one representative, how many electors does Washington, D.C., have in presidential and vice presidential elections? _____

AMENDMENT 24
Section 1
The right of citizens of the United States to vote in any primary or other election for President or Vice-President, for electors for President or Vice-President, or for senator or representative in Congress, shall not be denied or abridged by the United States or any state by reason of failure to pay any poll tax or other tax.

Section 2
The Congress shall have the power to enforce this article by appropriate legislation.

AMENDMENT 25
Section 1
In case of the removal of the President from office or of his death or resignation, the Vice-President shall become President.

Section 2
Whenever there is a vacancy in the office of the Vice-President, the President shall nominate a Vice-President who shall take office upon confirmation by a majority vote of both houses of Congress.

Section 3
Whenever the President transmits to the president pro tempore of the Senate and the Speaker of the House of Representatives his written declaration that he is unable to discharge the powers and duties of his office, and until he transmits to them a written declaration to the contrary, such powers and duties shall be discharged by the Vice-President as acting President.

Section 4
Whenever the Vice-President and majority of either the principal officers of the executive departments or of such other body as Congress may by law provide, transmit to the president pro tempore of the Senate and the speaker of the House of Representatives their written declaration that the President is unable to discharge the powers and duties of his office, the Vice-President shall immediately assume the powers and duties of the office as acting President.

Thereafter, when the President transmits to the president pro tempore of the Senate and the speaker of the House of Representatives his written declaration that no inability exists, he shall resume the powers and duties of his office unless the Vice-President and a majority of either the principal officers of the executive department or of such other body as Congress may by law provide, transmit within four days to the president pro tempore of the Senate and the speaker of the House of Representatives their written declaration that the President is unable to discharge the powers and duties of his office. Thereupon Congress shall decide the issue, assembling within forty-eight hours for that purpose if not in session. If the Congress, within twenty-one days after receipt of the latter written declaration, or, if Congress is not in session, within twenty-one days after Congress is required to assemble, determines by two-thirds vote of both houses that the President is unable to discharge the powers and duties of his office, the Vice-President shall continue to discharge the same as acting President; otherwise, the President shall resume the powers and duties of his office.

Historical Background

Before the Civil War, voters paid a fee to vote as a means of proving responsible citizenship. The practice became less honorable when, after the Civil War, Southern officials used the tax to prevent African Americans from voting. Almost a hundred years later, Amendment 24 was approved on January 23, 1964, making poll taxes illegal in federal primaries (a run-off election between candidates of the same party where the winner[s] move on to face the winner[s] of other parties' primaries in the general election) and federal elections.

The Constitution (Article 2, clause 6) fails to provide enough detail and leaves it up to Congress to decide situations when the president or vice president dies, becomes too ill, resigns, or is removed from office. Although the framers intended the vice president to serve only as a temporary replacement until a new election for president, Vice President Tyler demanded that he be sworn in as president in 1841 after Harrison became the first president to die in office. Since then, eight vice presidents have succeeded their presidents. Congress put this tradition in writing by proposing Amendment 25, which was approved on February 10, 1967. By allowing the president to name a successor, the amendment takes into account the fact that there had been 16 instances in the past when the office of vice president went unfilled until the next election. When Spiro Agnew resigned in 1973 because of bribe charges, President Nixon became the first president to use this power when he named Gerald Ford vice president. Congress approved and would later approve Ford's choice for the vice president after he succeeded Nixon, who also resigned, facing impeachment. Thus, for the first time in history, the United States had a vice president and president in office who were not elected by the people.

Know the Facts

Read Amendments 15-18 and fill in the blanks.

1. To vote, citizens do not have to pay a what? _____

2. Who becomes president when the president is removed, dies, or resigns or acts as president when the president cannot perform his or her duties? _____

3. Who approves vice presidential appointments to replace a vacancy? _____
   By what fraction of votes? _____

4. When there is disagreement on whether the president can return to his or her duties, who makes the final decision? _____ By what fraction of votes? _____

AMENDMENT 26
Section 1
The right of citizens of the United States, who are eighteen years of age or older, to vote shall not be denied or abridged by the United States or any state on account of age.

Section 2
The Congress shall have the power to enforce this article by appropriate legislation.

AMENDMENT 27
No law varying the compensation for the services of the senators and representatives shall take effect, until an election of representatives shall have intervened.

Historical Background

After World War II there was support to lower the voting age to eighteen when considering that a person could be drafted to fight for their country, yet not be old enough to vote. Support for the idea came full swing during the Vietnam War, and Amendment 26 was approved on July 1, 1971. In 1992, there was an effort to lower the voting age to 16.

As mentioned before, Amendment 27 was the original second amendment of 12 amendments submitted to states for approval as the Bill of Rights. Although not ratified at the time, it would be approved 203 years later because of Gregory Watson, a university student who wrote a paper in 1982 suggesting that the amendment could still be ratified. Ironically, his professor doubted the idea and gave him a C, but he never gave up. He led the effort, even spending his own money, until the amendment was approved on May 18, 1992. Some critics argued that the amendment needed to be proposed again by Congress to be valid. However, like the framers, supporters of today knew all too well the controversies surrounding officials giving themselves pay raises that took effect before the people had a chance to vote their opinion as to whether or not their congressman deserved to be reelected and see his or her pay raise.

Know the Facts

Answer the questions by filling in the blanks.

1. What is the minimum age required to vote? _____

2. When can a Congressional pay raise take effect? _____
_____

Practice Tests
Summarizing What You Have Read

Summarizing is an excellent way to help remember the general idea of a reading. Match the following summaries that best describe each article of the Constitution. The first one has been done.

1. __C__ Article I
2. _____ Article II
3. _____ Article III
4. _____ Article IV
5. _____ Article V
6. _____ Article VI
7. _____ Article VII

a. Reveals how to amend the Constitution
b. Explains the judicial branch
c. Explains the legislative branch
d. Explains the executive branch
e. Details ratification requirements
f. Describes federal supremacy and constitutional oath
g. Describes states' relations with one another and with the federal government

Match each of the ten summaries to the sections in Article I.

1. _____ Article I, Section 1
2. _____ Article I, Section 2
3. _____ Article I, Section 3
4. _____ Article I, Section 4
5. _____ Article I, Section 5
6. _____ Article I, Section 6
7. _____ Article I, Section 7
8. _____ Article I, Section 8
9. _____ Article I, Section 9
10. _____ Article I, Section 10

a. Powers of Congress
b. Congress, a two-house legislature
c. Congress rules, procedures, and duties
d. Powers denied to states
e. The House of Representatives
f. Congress elections and meetings
g. Congress benefits and restrictions
h. Procedures for bills and resolutions
i. Powers denied to Congress
j. The Senate

Articles II, III, IV, and VI

Match each of the 13 descriptions to the sections in Articles II, III, IV, and VI.

1. _____ Article II, Section 1
2. _____ Article II, Section 2
3. _____ Article II, Section 3
4. _____ Article II, Section 4
5. _____ Article III, Section 1
6. _____ Article III, Section 2
7. _____ Article III, Section 3
8. _____ Article IV, Section 1
9. _____ Article IV, Section 2
10. _____ Article IV, Section 3
11. _____ Article IV, Section 4
12. _____ Article VI, Section 1
13. _____ Article VI, Section 2
14. _____ Article VI, Section 3

a. Powers of the president
b. Citizen privileges and rights, extradition
c. Impeachment
d. Federal government guarantees to the states
e. Judicial power, federal courts, life terms, compensation
f. Constitution and national laws supreme
g. Executive power, terms, qualifications, elections, succession, salary, oath
h. Admission of new states and territories
i. Presidential duties, relationship to Congress
j. Oath of office
k. Full faith and credit of state acts and records
l. Treason defined
m. Federal court jurisdiction, trial by jury
n. Previous debts honored

The Amendments

Match each of the 27 summaries to the Constitution's amendments.

a. Selling, making, and shipping of liquor is illegal.
b. No forced housing of troops in people's homes.
c. Presidential and vice presidential candidates are elected by the electoral college.
d. People have basic rights not listed in the Constitution.
e. Congressional pay raises do not take effect until after an election of Representatives.
f. Legal age to vote is lowered to 18.
g. Right to speedy trial, lawyer, why arrested, to question and urge witnesses to testify.
h. The right to vote cannot be denied for reasons of race, color, or if formerly a slave.
i. Slavery is illegal.
j. Freedom of religion, speech, press, gather peaceably, and ask the government for help.
k. Right to trial by jury, due process, remain silent, and avoid double jeopardy.
l. Senators are directly elected by the people.
m. Right to trial by jury in noncriminal/civil cases.
n. Poll taxes are illegal.
o. Women can vote.
p. No state can be sued in federal court by a resident of another state or foreign country.
q. President succession.
r. Beginning terms of Congress and president changed; president elect succession.
s. A good reason and in most cases, a warrant, is needed to search and seize people's property.
t. Right to own guns and have state militias.
u. Protects from unfair bail, high fines, and cruel and unusual punishment.
v. Allows Congress to collect personal income taxes.
w. District of Columbia citizens can vote in presidential elections and has three electoral votes.
x. Federal ban on selling, manufacturing, and shipping of liquor removed.
y. The laws must be equally applied to U.S. citizens who are all guaranteed due process.
z. The states and people have powers not listed or forbidden in the Constitution.
aa. The president can serve only two terms.

1. ____ Amendment 1
2. ____ Amendment 2
3. ____ Amendment 3
4. ____ Amendment 4
5. ____ Amendment 5
6. ____ Amendment 6
7. ____ Amendment 7
8. ____ Amendment 8
9. ____ Amendment 9
10. ____ Amendment 10
11. ____ Amendment 11
12. ____ Amendment 12
13. ____ Amendment 13
14. ____ Amendment 14
15. ____ Amendment 15
16. ____ Amendment 16
17. ____ Amendment 17
18. ____ Amendment 18
19. ____ Amendment 19
20. ____ Amendment 20
21. ____ Amendment 21
22. ____ Amendment 22
23. ____ Amendment 23
24. ____ Amendment 24
25. ____ Amendment 25
26. ____ Amendment 26
27. ____ Amendment 27

Knowing the Vocabulary

Try defining the following terms without looking them up on their listed page. The first one is completed as an example.

1. Indirect Democracy (1) __A type of democracy in which the people elect representatives to make laws and national decisions for them.__

2. Constitution (1) _____

3. Liberty (7) _____

4. Impeachment (8) _____

5. Veto (16) _____

6. Necessary and Proper Clause (19) _____

7. Writ of Habeas Corpus (20) _____

8. Bill of Attainder (20) _____

9. Ex Post Facto Law (20) _____

10. Judicial Review (27) _____

11. Federalism (28) _____

12. Separation of Powers (28) _____

13. Checks and Balances (28) _____

14. Republican Government (30) _____

15. Supremacy Clause (32) _____

16. Double Jeopardy (37) _____

17. Electoral College (39) _____

CRITICAL THINKING QUESTIONS

Using what you have learned about the Constitution's rules and history, answer the following questions by trying to infer the framers' reasoning behind the following rules or concepts.

1. When the president has been impeached and is on trial, why does the chief justice of the Supreme Court control the trial and not the vice president, who oversees all other impeachment trials?

2. Why is a quorum needed to conduct legislative business?

3. Why must bills to raise money start in the House of Representatives?

4. Why is it important for Congress to make trade rules and not the states?

5. Why do congressmen and the president have different term lengths?

6. Why was the Constitution made the highest law of the land?

7. Why have voting requirements been changed over the years?

8. What major problem is avoided by only requiring a majority, two-thirds, or three-fourths vote and not a unanimous vote?

Sample Practice Exam

Test your memory by selecting the best answer as shown in the first question.

__C__ 1. House of Representatives are chosen how often?
   a. life time appointment   b. 4 years   c. 2 years   d. 6 years

___ 2. To be a House member, what is the minimum age requirements?
   a. 25 years   b. 20 years   c. 30 years   d. 35 years

___ 3. Which house sits as a court and "tries" impeachments?
   a. Senate   b. Parliament   c. Supreme Court   d. House

___ 4. Which house has the power of impeachment?
   a. Senate   b. House   c. Parliament   d. Supreme Court

___ 5. Each state has how many senators?
   a. 4   b. 3   c. 2   d. 1

___ 6. What is the length of a senator's term?
   a. 2 years   b. 4 years   c. 8 years   d. 6 years

___ 7. What is the minimum citizenship requirements to be a House member?
   a. 5 years   b. 7 years   c. 9 years   d. 14 years

___ 8. What is the minimum citizenship requirements to be a senator?
   a. 2 years   b. 7 years   c. 9 years   d. 14 years

___ 9. To be a senator, what is the minimum age requirements?
   a. 30 years   b. 25 years   c. 20 years   d. 35 years

___ 10. How many days does the president have to veto a bill before it automatically becomes a law?
   a. 5 days   b. 7 days   c. 10 days   d. 15 days

___ 11. How long is a presidential term?
   a. 4 years   b. 2 years   c. 6 years   d. 8 years

___ 12. What is the minimum age requirements to be the president?
   a. 30 years   b. 25 years   c. 21 years   d. 35 years

___ 13. This group of 14 advises the president and is called what?
   a. Congress   b. cabinet   c. Supreme Court   d. full committee

___ 14. This power allows the Supreme Court to declare laws unconstitutional.
   a. Supremacy Power   b. Elastic Power   c. Amending Power   d. Judicial Review

___ 15. This clause allows Congress to make all needed laws.
    a. Supremacy Clause   b. Elastic Clause   c. Amending Clause   d. Judicial Review

___ 16. This clause says the Constitution is the law of the land.
    a. Elastic   b. Santa   c. Supremacy   d. Judicial

___ 17. Who has the power to make treaties and send troops into battle?
    a. Senators   b. Representatives   c. chief justice   d. president

___ 18. Who must approve treaties?
    a. Senate   b. House   c. chief justice   d. president

___ 19. Who can declare a treaty unconstitutional?
    a. Senate   b. House   c. president   d. Supreme Court

___ 20. Who has the power to appoint Supreme Courts judges?
    a. Senate   b. House   c. Supreme Court   d. president

___ 21. Who approves Supreme Court appointments?
    a. Senate   b. House   c. president   d. Supreme Court

___ 22. Where do bills to raise money originate?
    a. Senate   b. House   c. Supreme Court   d. president

___ 23. Who ratifies a Constitutional amendment?
    a. states   b. president   c. Congress   d. Supreme Court

___ 24. An amendment to the Constitution must be ratified by what fraction?
    a. ½   b. ⅔   c. ⅕   d. ¾

___ 25. When not at a convention for this purpose, who proposes amendments and has the power to declare war?
    a. Congress   b. states   c. president   d. Supreme Court

___ 26. What fraction is needed for a proposed amendment to move on to the next step?
    a. ½   b. ⅓   c. ⅔   d. ¾

___ 27. How many judges are there currently on the Supreme Court?
    a. 8   b. 10   c. 7   d. 9

___ 28. By what fraction must Congress vote to overturn a presidential veto?
    a. ¾   b. ⅔   c. $22/7$ d. ½

___ 29. How many senators and representatives are there total?
    a. $101/437 = 538$ b. $50/235 = 285$ c. $200/345 = 545$ d. $100/435 = 535$

ANSWER KEY

Pre-Colonial Background
1. E
2. A
3. F
4. B
5. D
6. C

Pre-Revolution Background — Page 3
1. B
2. D
3. A
4. C
5. E

Revolution, Independence, and First Government — Page 4
1. C
2. A
3. D
4. B

Steps to a New Government — Page 5
1. D
2. C
3. B
4. A

How the Constitution Is Organized — Page 7
A. 3
B. 5
C. 1
D. 4
E. 6
F. 2

Vocabulary Matching
A. 10
B. 4
C. 8
D. 13
E. 17
F. 1
G. 11
H. 2
I. 7
J. 3
K. 15
L. 5
M. 18
N. 16
O. 12
P. 6
Q. 9
R. 14

Know the Facts
1. C
2. E and F
3. A
4. B
5. D and K
6. H and J
7. G
8. I

Vocabulary Matching — Page 10
A. 2
B. 6
C. 8
D. 1
E. 12
F. 4
G. 15
H. 14
I. 7
J. 9
K. 11
L. 3
M. 10
N. 13
O. 5

Know the Facts — Page 11
1. H
2. E
3. B
4. J
5. A
6. F
7. C
8. I
9. K
10. G
11. L
12. D

Vocabulary Matching — Page 12
A. 16
B. 7
C. 14
D. 5
E. 12
F. 4
G. 10
H. 2
I. 8
J. 15
K. 6
L. 13
M. 1
N. 11
O. 3
P. 9

Know the Facts — Page 13
Corrections to false answers may vary slightly.
1. 0, Congress must meet at least once a year.
2. 0, A majority (quorum) is needed to make laws.
3. +
4. 0, Only one fifth need approve.
5. +
6. 0, State legislatures, not Congress, make election laws.
7. 0, A two-thirds vote is needed to remove a member.
8. +

Vocabulary Matching — Page 15
A. 4
B. 6
C. 1
D. 18
E. 3
F. 8
G. 15
H. 12
I. 16
J. 5
K. 7
L. 10
M. 2
N. 9
O. 14
P. 13
Q. 17
R. 11

Know the Facts — Page 15
1. L
2. P
3. P
4. L

How a Bill Becomes a Law — Page 16
A. 6
B. 1
C. 7
D. 2
E. 4
F. 3
G. 5

The Powers of Congress — Page 17
1. laws
2. investigate
3. impeach
4. vetoes
5. treaties
6. money
7. tax
8. trade
9. citizen
10. bankruptcy
11. weights
12. felony
13. post
14. science, arts
15. copyrights
16. courts
17. war
18. armed
19. militias
20. land

Vocabulary Matching, Part I — Page 19
A. 15
B. 13
C. 11
D. 9
E. 7
F. 5
G. 3
H. 1
I. 2
J. 14
K. 12
L. 10
M. 8
N. 6
O. 4

Vocabulary Matching, Part II — Page 19
A. 22
B. 17
C. 21
D. 18
E. 30
F. 28
G. 25
H. 27
I. 26
J. 16
K. 19
L. 20
M. 23
N. 29
O. 24

Vocabulary Matching — Page 21
A. 7
B. 5
C. 8
D. 3
E. 11
F. 1
G. 13
H. 17
I. 15
J. 6
K. 4
L. 2
M. 9
N. 12
O. 10
P. 14
Q. 16

© Instructional Fair • TS Denison

IF2738 The Constitution

Know the Facts — Page 21
A. 6
B. 4
C. 7
D. 2
E. 8
F. 1
G. 5
H. 3

Vocabulary Matching — Page 22
A. 11
B. 6
C. 12
D. 3
E. 1
F. 7
G. 5
H. 2
I. 10
J. 9
K. 4
L. 8

Know the Facts — Page 22
1. treaties
2. alliances
3. confederations
4. money
5. nobility titles
6. letters of marque and reprisal
7. bills of attainder
8. ex post facto laws
9. laws impairing contracts

Know the Facts — Page 24
1. 4 years
2. no
3. electors
4. citizen, 35 years, 14 years
5. vice president

Powers of the President — Page 24
1. Chief Executive
2. Commander in Chief
3. keep advisors
4. grant pardons, reprieves
5. make treaties, appointments
6. recommend laws
7. Head of State

Vocabulary Matching — Page 25
A. 5
B. 3
C. 1
D. 7
E. 4
F. 2
G. 8
H. 6

Vocabulary Matching — Page 27
A. 7
B. 12
C. 6
D. 16
E. 1
F. 5
G. 15
H. 11
I. 8
J. 4
K. 13
L. 9
M. 3
N. 14
O. 2
P. 10

Know the Facts — Page 27
1. the Supreme Court
2. Congress
3. life terms
4. President, Senate, 2/3
5. Supreme Court
6. trial by jury
7. treason

Separating, Checking, and Balancing the Powers — Page 28
Legislative over Judicial—D, L, F
Judicial over Legislative—C
Judicial over Executive—H, M
Executive over Judicial—E, N
Legislative over Executive—I, O, B, K, G
Executive over Legislative—P, J, A

Limiting the Powers — Page 29
1. L, S
2. E
3. J
4. L, R
5. E
6. L, R
7. L, S
8. E
9. L, S, R
10. J
11. L, S
12. E
13. E
14. L, R

Vocabulary Matching — Page 31
A. 10
B. 7
C. 11
D. 4
E. 1
F. 9
G. 2
H. 3
I. 6
J. 8
K. 5

Know the Facts — Page 31
1. the states
2. full faith and credit
3. Section 2, clause 1
4. treason, felony, other crime
5. state executive authority (governor)
6. slaves
7. Congress
8. republican form
9. invasion and domestic violence

Vocabulary Matching — Page 33
A. 9
B. 4
C. 2
D. 7
E. 1
F. 5
G. 10
H. 6
I. 3
J. 8

Know the Facts — Page 33
1. Congress, state conventions, 2/3
2. the states, 3/4
3. the equal number of senators allowed to each state
4. U.S. Constitution
5. religious test

Vocabulary Matching — Page 35
A. 9
B. 7
C. 2
D. 3
E. 5
F. 4
G. 1
H. 6
I. 8

Know the Facts — Page 35
1. freedom of religion, speech, press, gather peaceably, and ask the government for help
2. the right to own guns and have a state militia
3. no forced housing of troops in people's homes
4. a good reason is needed to search and seize people's property; a warrant

Vocabulary Matching — Page 37
A. 12
B. 15
C. 11
D. 1
E. 3
F. 14
G. 9
H. 4
I. 17
J. 2
K. 13
L. 5
M. 18
N. 10
O. 8
P. 6
Q. 7
R. 16

Know the Facts — Page 37
A. 9
B. 5
C. 6
D. 6
E. 6
F. 8
G. 5
H. 6
I. 6
J. 10
K. 5
L. 6
M. 8
N. 5
O. 7

Vocabulary Matching — Page 39
A. 2
B. 4
C. 9
D. 7
E. 3
F. 6
G. 10
H. 8
I. 5
J. 1

Know the Facts — Page 39
1. citizens from other states and foreign countries
2. House of Representatives, Senate
3. no
4. slavery

Vocabulary Matching — Page 41
A. 1
B. 3
C. 2
D. 4
E. 6
F. 5
G. 7

Know the Facts — Page 41
1. those U.S.-born and naturalized
2. due process of law
3. equal protection of the laws

Know the Facts — Page 43
1. race, color, or if formerly a slave
2. taxes
3. senator
4. selling, making, and shipping of liquor

Know the Facts — Page 45
1. sex
2. women
3. January 20
4. January 3
5. to prevent "lame ducks"
6. Vice President Elect

Know the Facts — Page 47
1. repeals Amendment 18
2. the states
3. by state convention
4. two terms
5. ten years
6. three electors

Know the Facts — Page 49
1. poll tax
2. vice president
3. Congress, majority
4. Congress, 2/3

Know the Facts — Page 50
1. 18 years of age
2. after an election for House of Representatives

Summarizing What You Have Read — Page 51
1. C
2. D
3. B
4. G
5. A
6. F
7. E

1. B
2. E
3. J
4. F
5. C
6. G
7. H
8. A
9. I
10. D

Articles II, III, IV, and VI — Page 52
1. G
2. A
3. I
4. C
5. E
6. M
7. L
8. K
9. B
10. H
11. D
12. N
13. F
14. J

Page 53
1. j
2. t
3. b
4. s
5. k
6. g
7. m
8. u
9. d
10. z
11. p
12. c
13. i
14. y
15. h
16. v
17. l
18. a
19. o
20. r
21. x
22. aa
23. w
24. n
25. q
26. f
27. e

Knowing the Vocabulary — Page 54
1. a type of democracy in which the people elect representatives to make laws and national decisions for them
2. a set of written rules that describes and defines the government's purpose, principle, powers, limits, organization, and relationship between the government and the people governed
3. freedoms, independence
4. to accuse a federal official of a crime or wrongdoing in the House of Representatives; the Senate convicts
5. to reject a bill or resolution
6. gives Congress the flexibility and power to pass any laws needed to carry out its duties
7. a legal paper requiring a jailed person be charged with a crime or be released
8. a law that punishes a group or person without a trial
9. a law that punishes the accused for something done before the law was passed
10. the power to declare a law, treaty, or executive action unconstitutional
11. a system of government in which a Constitution defines how governmental powers are shared and divided between a national and regional/state governments
12. powers of government divided and limited among three independent and coequal branches: legislative, executive, and judicial
13. To prevent abuses, each branch uses its power to check the actions and powers of the other two branches and achieve a balance of power.
14. a government run by representatives chosen by the people
15. a rule that says the U.S. Constitution is the highest law of the land; all other laws must agree with the Constitution.
16. tried twice for the same crime even if found innocent after the first trial
17. the process by which candidates are chosen to be president and vice president by state electors

Critical Thinking Questions — Page 55
Answers may vary slightly.
1. to avoid possible unfair treatment since the vice president would become the next president if the president were convicted
2. A majority should always be present to best represent the nation's views and, thus, prevent the nation from being controlled by only a few.
3. Representatives have always been chosen by the people and, therefore, the states with more population and the people as a whole, control taxation.
4. Under the Articles of Confederation, the states made unfair competitive trade rules.
5. Differing terms promote separation of powers, holding elected officials accountable to new officials chosen by the people.
6. Some set of laws had to be held supreme to prevent the central government or the states from abusing their powers.
7. Although voting requirements were left up to the states, the framers generally thought it best that white males, over 21, and with property only vote since they had a vested interest in preventing government abuses. Over time it became necessary to prevent white males from abusing their power.
8. A unanimous vote/total agreement requires too much time or is impossible to achieve on many issues. Although it is less democratic since the minority often loses out, it is viewed as the best way to get things done.

Sample Practice Exam — Pages 56-57
1. c
2. a
3. a
4. b
5. c
6. d
7. b
8. c
9. a
10. c
11. a
12. d
13. b
14. d
15. b
16. c
17. d
18. a
19. d
20. d
21. a
22. b
23. a
24. d
25. a
26. c
27. d
28. b
29. d